NOTHING VANISHES

Memoir of a Life Transformed

Karen Lauritzen

SWEET
WOODS
PRESS

Published by Sweet Woods Press, PO Box 12,
Brevard, NC, 28712-0012
Printed in the United States of America

Copyright © 2012 by Karen Lauritzen

The following stories from this book have been previously
published elsewhere. "Nothing Vanishes" in *The Chrysalis
Reader* and "Seat 7F" in *Kaleidoscope Magazine: Exploring the
Experience of Disability Through the Fine Arts*".

Quotations on pages 126 and 141 are by May Sarton.

Karen Lauritzen 1943--
ISBN 978-0-9858595-0-3
Library of Congress Control Number: 2012950763

Book cover, interior design and imprint by Ginger Graziano
www.gingergraziano.com
Cover photograph by Pamela Blevins
Dragonfly image by Shutterstock

To my sons, John and Jason, who took me places
I never would have traveled on my own.

To my partner Everett for his patience and belief in me.

To my extended Italian family out there—*Grazie mille!*

I wish I could say that there are no ghosts in my family cemetery, but that, of course, would be a lie. I don't tell many people about this, at least, not until they know me well, know that I am a just-the-facts-ma'am kind of person and that what I write is grounded, real, solid, visible. I don't want people thinking: *She's gone over the edge.* You get what I am saying. *So I will tell you.* I will tell you because you know me well enough to know that what I say is the truth: *I wish I could say there are no ghosts at the top of the hill on my property, but that's just not so.*

It's like this: when I created the cemetery at the highest point on my land, I wasn't thinking. I was grieving, mourning the loss of my husband and friend of twenty-two years, the father of our two children who were then eight and twelve years old. Just children, needing me, and needing him close by.

Sweet Woods Garden. That is what I called the place he was buried. I dug a circle of plants to surround the barren red clay and scrabbled grass that graced the ground over his grave. I believed the closer I got to the earth, the faster I would heal.

In my mind I was preparing yet another place of residence, a place of residence for my husband, Henry, and for the others who followed, two aunts and both parents, one death every two years during the next ten years. I simply was making other housing arrangements for them, not really different from all the other plans I'd made: assisted living, nursing home, hospital, hospice.

I wasn't thinking. I was reacting, wide-open, knee-jerk, right-brain stuff. I had sent my left brain, the logical, rational, objective part of me, somewhere else.

All that right-brain thinking has led me to where I am today, living a life where ghosts govern. My dreams are full of messages, not of *my* choosing, but *theirs.* If I ignore them, all the next day there's a flash in the corner of my eye that pulls me abruptly from whatever I'm doing to stand at the front door and look toward the cemetery.

So who is it now?

"I'LL TAKE THAT ONE," I pointed to the blue coaster bike with fat tires and wide silver fenders sitting like a chubby lady beside the slender, three- five- and ten- speeds. A salesman at the register looked up from his paperwork, "The coaster bike, eh?"

"Yep. That one."

"Well, now," he stepped away from the register, "We've got a sale on three-speeds. Great for negotiating Chicago traffic." He paused in his sales pitch and looked at me.

"Nope. Just that one." I nodded at the coaster bike and walked toward it. I ran my right hand across the wide, black seat, and felt the soft padding bounce against my palm. *Comfortable.* "I don't need anything fancy. Just something for shopping. I'll put a basket on the front." *How do riders balance on the narrow tires of those skinny bikes, perched high above the turned-down handle bars on that tiny seat like birds on a branch? Not me.*

The salesman looked at me straightway, "Hey, I'm Hank or Henry. Some call me 'Henry Hank'." His right hand reached forward for a handshake. That's when I felt the tingle, the charge, as his fingers encircled mine. Then I noticed him, really noticed him.

"Oh. I'm Karen." *I wish I'd dressed in something nicer than jeans and a long-sleeved, slightly frumpy, white shirt.* I stepped back to regain my composure. *I didn't expect this. I didn't expect*

*to find him in Morrie Mages Sporting Goods at eleven o'clock on a
Sunday morning.*

"Well. No, really. Just a coaster bike." He grinned, placing
the long, slender fingers of those great-looking hands on his hips.
The rest of him was scruffy. His hair needed a trim, his shirt
could have used ironing, his shoes a coat of polish, *but his hands.
He's got great hands! His nails are clipped and smooth, his palm wide
enough to give the world a solid grasp. It's been a long time since a
man held me, really held me. Those hands will do just fine!*

"You seem to know what you want."

"Yep."

"All the time?"

"Most of the time."

"Well, then, it's the one for you."

I stared at him. *Did I just hear "it's the one" or "I'm the one"?* I
shifted from one foot to the other. Then, finding nothing more
creative to do to hide my continuing awkwardness, I looked
back at the bike. *Maybe he thinks I'm a nerd for buying a clunky
coaster bike. Shit!*

"How do you want to pay for this?"

I handed him my credit card and our hands touched again.
Another tingle. He bent down to do the paperwork and I noticed his blond hair, a little thin at the crown, but the rest of
him was fit and trim in chinos and a button-down shirt. He
stepped forward. Another tingle as he handed me the receipt.
"All yours."

"Ah, thanks for your help." *How do I draw out this conversation?* I couldn't get the words out: *How about dinner? A drink?*

Just last week, over cocktails, I had told my girlfriends: "I
want a man who sweeps me off my feet. I want to feel something
special, magical."

One of them replied, "Yeah, *right*. In about a million years! How about settling for a guy who is not gay and works?"

"Nope," I said. "I'm holding out for what I want his time." My first marriage had lasted eighteen months. The "white knight" was a "dark horse" with an even darker past. And after that marriage ended, well, I guess you could say I was untethered.

I HAVE NEVER BEEN in this room before. Where am I? My head! Ooh! I rolled onto my side and saw a man lying next to me. *Who is* he? *I need to get out of here! Where's my purse? Do I still have one? Have I got any money?*

Okay. I took a deep breath. *Pull yourself together.* I blinked grit from my eyes. Rubbed them.

He's snoring. Maybe that's what woke me. I slipped from the bed. Littered on the floor at my feet were my clothes. *At least I've got my clothes. I'll just, Oh! Work! Today is Monday. What time is it?* I peered at the bedside clock through puffy eyes. Eight o'clock. I needed to be at work in one hour.

Reflected in the bathroom mirror of this somebody's apartment was smeared makeup, caked eyeliner, disheveled hair. I rummaged through my purse which somehow had ended up on the bathroom floor. I found a twenty dollar bill, a stick of gum, my apartment key, a tube of Revlon "Ruby Red" lipstick, my driver's license and one maxed-out Visa card.

I rinsed my cottony mouth using the filmy glass from the sink, looked around the bathroom, found a washcloth and ran it across my face. *Sour! Ugh!* I opened the medicine cabinet. *Mouthwash, thank God.* I finger-combed my hair. I had no makeup except lipstick, but there was a number-two pencil in the medicine cabinet. I grabbed it and filled in my eyebrows. *Using a pencil made of graphite for eye make-up might be a bit toxic, but hey, after what I must have poured into my body last night. . . .*

I surveyed my image in the mirror over the sink. *Hmm, passable for work. I might get away with it if I don't stand too close to anyone.* I pulled on the lemon-yellow, leather miniskirt, matching vest and fitted, white turtleneck sweater I wore the night before. I stepped into black, knee-length, patent-leather boots. *If I can slip out of here before this guy wakes up. . . .*

I exited the lobby and stepped into the street to hail a cab. Thankfully I was on the near north side of Chicago and not many miles from work. It was morning rush hour and all passing cabs were full. *I can make it to work and back home on the twenty in my purse. The elevated will take too long and I'll get to work late and miss the staff meeting.*

Finally, a cab pulled over. "Madden Mental Health Center on Ogden, please, driver."

In the margin of the discarded *Chicago Tribune* on the seat next to me, I scribbled a few notes with the number-two pencil I purloined from that somebody's apartment, outlining what I can remember for the meeting I would be leading: "Crisis Intervention for Families with Members Who are Chronically Ill." I tried to concentrate but found my mind repeating a familiar conversation with myself.

Black Russian? Is that what I drank last night? I promised myself I would lay off the scotch. Vodka worked better and Black Russian looked like coffee when I carried it in my thermos to BYO parties.

Who am I kidding? This is insane, going out and picking up guys I don't even know and will never see again, putting my life on the line for a night of what? Oblivion? To pretend I am in a relationship? I talk to my clients about this all the time and suggest that they go to AA. What makes me think I'm different?

Back to my list. Today I am a good girly social worker taking care of others, fixing the broken places in their lives. Last night was just a dark cloud in this sunny social worker's life.

The cab arrived at eight fifty-five. I smoothed the front of my miniskirt, fluffed my hair, took a deep breath and put on my *Enough* face. I pushed open the door to the clinic, smiled at my boss, the clinic administrator, and gave him my I've-got-it-under-control look.

He looked back at me and gave me the fish eye. "This is the new look for clinical social workers at the Department of Mental Health?"

COME ON! SAY SOMETHING clever! I was twenty-nine-years old but felt as clumsy as I did on my first date. "Well, bye." *Is that your best shot? No wonder you spend so much time home alone!*

I pushed my new coaster bike out the door and along the sidewalk on La Salle Street. "Damn!" I muttered under my breath. *Missed opportunity.* Maybe I could return in a couple of days and purchase some accessories, a lock, a key, a basket. *But how will I know what his work schedule is? Damn! Damn! Damn!* I tugged at my shirt, straightening the hem, as if adjusting my clothing would make any difference.

"Karen, wait up!" Henry Hank waved at me, one hand on the turned-down handlebars of the lightest-weight, white, Italian bike I had ever seen. He was pushing one of those ridiculously uncomfortable, raised, seat-on-a-post ten-speeds, sidling up to my flat-lander. "Maybe I ought to ride with you for a while. You know, just to make sure you can manage that thing." He looked down at the sidewalk, avoiding my gaze, and suddenly seemed as shy and awkward as I.

"Sure! Okay!"

"I've got the rest of the day off," he volunteered. "Maybe we'll work up an appetite riding. May I buy you lunch? A drink?"

"Lunch sounds good. But I'm not drinking right now. I'm cutting back on calories."

THE TRUST WE FORGED formed the bond that carried our marriage through the years. For the next twenty-two years we weren't apart much. We rode our bikes along Chicago's Lakefront, made a life for ourselves, had two children, always talking, planning, never without something to say to each other and the spark never dimmed.

Until he died.

Now, fifteen years after his death, I still miss his companionship, our history. I long to have the final conversation we never had. I am certain that the vague, blurry figure that's been flashing past my vision at the top of the hill in Sweet Woods Garden is Henry.

My bedroom is always kept pitch black at night, save tiny pinpricks of light creeping through slits in the blinds. Inky black is what I need for sleep. I am light-sensitive and the smallest flicker rouses me from sound sleep. I open my eyes. Too early. The air above me whirs and spins like an out-of-control ceiling fan. My eyes pop open ahead of my sluggish brain and I struggle to orient myself. *Now what? Who's calling me?*

I sit upright in bed. They are at it again, pulling me from the warmth of my bed to walk through the wet grass to the family cemetery. I shake my head and smile as I dress, knowing that my body, warm from sleep, in moments will feel cold, damp. *Just like them*, but not really. I know that the spirits who rise from five graves no longer embody pain or pleasure, at least, not like I do. Yet here they are, interfering with my comfort.

I cared for all of them until they died and I buried them in Sweet Woods Garden with the thought that they would *Rest in Peace* and so would I. I thought I would have time to do what I wanted once their bodies no longer needed care and attention. *It almost seems as if I have been tricked, foiled by my filial affection for them. They took so much of my time when they were alive and now they are robbing me of one of my great pleasures, a good night's sleep.*

I know that if I ignore these urgings further messages will include disturbance of the cemetery grounds. Grass will stop growing or the border of pea gravel around markers will be thrown around. They will get my attention. I have learned that rising when they call is, in the long run, less effort, less garden labor, than ignoring them.

But this time, there is a new presence. Something different. The flickering at the corner of my eye had been going on for days. A figure would appear, then fade from my vision. I was busy. I ignored it.

They were impatient. *I had best get up there. Go to them. Let them have their say. Especially Henry.*

The flow of energy around my body shifts and I begin to distinguish night from day, consciousness from dreaming. The image of that same form appears as I walk out the front door toward the cemetery. This dawn he is coming toward me, to the black, wrought-iron gate of Sweet Woods Garden. He is the same man with the broad shoulders and long arms and big hands, those hands that caressed my body as we conceived two sons all those years ago.

I see his hand press open the latch on the gate. *I want to touch you one last time. Talk about that last day. Tell you about the boys, my life. Stay! Wait!* I want to run to him but my feet won't move.

I stand frozen in the mist and can hardly breathe, afraid if I exhale the whoosh from my breath will be enough to blow away his misty form. I see him look away from me down at the pattern of laurel leaves forged into the gate design, the laurel that owns the property here. He smiles. *Oh, my!* I touch my hand to my racing heart and my breath catches. *He is pleased with my choice.* I had not known he liked my design for the gate, but how could I? He died before it was conceived.

In the early dawn light, the flat, brass markers glow like mirrors against the starlit sky, reflecting the planets almost as if they are reaching for their place in space.

He comes toward me. He walks through the gate, crosses the top of the hill and continues toward me, to the house, *our house.*

I REMEMBER HIS WORDS when we bought the house on Grand-view Drive: "You will have to live it out." We paid more for it than he had wanted to spend and he told me I would have to stay, live in it until I would make a profit.

I agreed to his terms. *Anything* to get him settled. He was ill.

When we could no longer keep his illness in check, we made this desperate move from broad-shouldered Chicago, the city we loved for years, to North Carolina, to live in a gentler climate cradled in the misty foothills of the Blue Ridge Mountains. He knew what was happening to his body then. I watched as he grew quieter, thinner. I watched his life dim and flicker, the light leaving the edges of his eyes. This property would become more my place, the boys' place, than his.

His focus had always been on worth. "A house is an emotional investment, honey," he told me, calculator in hand. But I knew he bought the house because he liked it, too, and wouldn't be a renter beholden to a landlord, left only with a stack of rent receipts at the end of the tax year. He ran his fingers across the line on the mortgage document, tracing the word "Owner" with his index finger: "Ours. We're in the North Carolina tax system now."

He pulled the white van we had driven from Chicago to the top of the hill the day we moved in. "Well, now, that's one beautiful view," he said, gazing at the panorama of the Blue Ridge Mountains from the highest elevation of our property. "I'd like to be buried here." This statement, the first acknowledgment of his mortality since we had met, slipped from his lips like a last request.

The hazy figure I see still walks with that strength I love, that knowing force, the intention of a focused man. He brought all of his physical presence to whatever he did and since he was a big man, his size covered the lack of surety I carried in my small frame.

I have been to Sweet Woods Garden often in the past weeks. Writing. Thinking. Watching. I've felt something. *Something.*

The wind is up and rustles the crape myrtle and dogwood leaves that are just beginning to bud. I feel the force of it all, the wind and the stars, the new buds. The azaleas around the base of the bench where I often sit reach to the sky. Miniature rose bushes brush against my bare legs scratching them, competing for my attention. The dogwood seems taller, as if it is growing in the night energy. This early dawn I am aware of my earthbound feet, my earthbound self, as everything around me focuses upward.

There's a sense of foreboding in the air. I feel I am being watched by silent, quiet eyes at the edge of the nearby woods. But this is my safe place and I shrug my shoulders to discard the feeling. *There it is again.* I know another pair of eyes is watching. My body tenses; my shoulders hunch and my neck tightens. I can't quite relax. Not this time.

ALL THE DAY BEFORE, I had stood at the front door staring at the cemetery gate, wondering, distracted. *Just who is that flashing past my eye?* The figure was a blur, indistinct. *There, then gone.* A hazy outline of broad shoulders, a big man with long arms, in beige pants and a long-sleeved blue shirt. *Could it be?*

I had not seen him appear before and he had been dead fifteen years. *But it is his birthday week. Now, he would just be the one to do that! Use an occasion to show up and mark it with his unique signature, just like the day the four of us, Henry, me, and the boys, John and Jason, posed for a family photo.*

"Let's get the picture taken before the boys outgrow their new dress clothes," I said. So we all posed dressed in white clothes from a recent vacation. Then, at the last minute, Henry pinned his World War II victory medal on the lapel of his white dinner jacket, a shiny brass pin with red and blue ribbons. It stood out like an advertisement against his white blazer. I had not seen the medal before. He never mentioned it and he never wore it. That medal got more attention once we hung the finished, framed photo than the carefully pressed dress clothes and neatly groomed kids. He sure knew how to keep me from taking life too seriously.

I'M HERE. I WILL LISTEN. Yet the message is indistinct, a foreboding, a foreshadowing, and the image of his tall, square frame fades again in the moonlight.

Don't go, don't go. My fingers ball into a hard fist.

I walk back across the top of the hill through the yard under the beech trees and see a red fox (the other pair of eyes that's been watching me) dart back into the thicket, his dawn patrol disturbed by my wandering. The fox thinks outside the box, has drive and desire and strategies for survival, not unlike the figure at the gate.

As HIS ENERGIES DWINDLED, he became uncommonly silent, settling into a part of himself he rarely showed anyone but me. Our closest friends chided me, "Honestly! I just talked to him. He sounds great. He said he was okay." One of my step children called, "He's really alright. I know *my* Dad. *You* worry too much!"

His kids and our friends thought I was overprotective. But they didn't get it because they couldn't know. He *had* to leave the cold Chicago winters, the full-time-plus responsibility of running the manufacturing plant he and his partner owned. The wintertime trips to the hospital for infections had become all too frequent and he was never a man who would wear a surgical mask to protect his immune system.

"Come on," I told him a few months after we moved into our new home. "I'll teach you how." We walked down the back road toward the pond full of fish on our neighbor's property. I carried a folding chair, a cane pole, and showed him how to bait the hook and toss it into the shallow pond. "Just stay away from the floating grasses and water lilies. You'll snag your line." He fished one time and the photo of him, pole in hand, taken two months before he died, joined other photos on the family room bookshelf. I made copies of it, sent it to our friends. "So you are finally getting him to relax," they said.

Henry didn't talk much about his illness after he shared his diagnosis. "It's a long-term thing," he told his four grown children from his first marriage and our two sons. "I've got another eleven years, they tell me, on the outside." His focus was his reclaimed self, the whole person he had become after emerging from the shattered man he had been following the divorce from his first wife. He had spent years repairing ruptured relationships with his four kids caused by the end of that marriage. He wanted the best of himself given over to them. He said he was never going back to feeling broken again.

He was the guy who convinced everyone he was invincible, from his "Captain America" red, white and blue, save-the-world swim trunks, to starting a business at fifty, to running a half marathon in celebration of his fifty-third birthday, to having a second family. He delighted his grandchildren from his first marriage by removing the hairpiece he wore, then his front teeth (really a dental bridge), and finally, reaching toward his right eye, saying: "Wanna see that come out, too?" He left the grandchildren screaming with delight, amazed he could remove, then replace, body parts. It helped him sell the story and they bought the story he sold. They minimized a fatal illness because he did. They all believed this super salesman had superpowers.

What few saw was the fatigue, the listlessness, the exhaustion. When his body temperature dropped suddenly he wore a natty gold blazer rather than old-guy undershirts or turtlenecks so he still looked good as he drove the sleek, black company-leased Mercedes eight blocks to the coffee shop downtown. No one but me saw how many nights he slept in a recliner or the days he took naps. No one but me made the frenetic drives to a hospital forty minutes away when a sudden fever overcame him. No one else was there to plead with him not to leave the hospital against medical advice. No one heard him mutter under his breath like a mantra, "I can beat this."

Now it seems that Henry will be like the others. I had seen four figures bathed in light, looking like photos in a family album, undeniable and familiar as the back of my hand. I wanted to ignore them, get on with my life, but they are my family and I cannot deny this link, this blood bond. Not possible, not with my history. Not everyone would understand, maybe a highly intuitive person, a Native American Indian or one of my aunts who was born in Italy and spent her childhood praying in an eight-hundred-year-old Catholic Church where the bones of the saints were buried beneath the sacristy. *La famiglia,* the family, that's what I believe in. That is what holds my life together. So I stand at the window gaping at the familiar forms, looking at ghosts, talking to ghosts. Wondering when they will appear, knowing they never choose a time that doesn't turn my life upside down, leaving me teeter-tottering between two worlds.

I shake my head, and smile, remembering. In their nineties, my aunts who are buried in Sweet Woods Garden traveled from Arkansas to a family reunion in North Carolina and never left. They moved into an assisted living center not five minutes from my home. If I didn't visit them early each day, I would receive a call by two in the afternoon, "Are you coming?" There was that expectation of attention. Giving my time, that part of myself they knew was their due. Honoring them. Attention to them on a daily basis was part of the contract and it was mandatory, *required.*

How do I know that when I buried them on my property I agreed to a continuation of that contract? It is a complex network of unspoken promises. And it's binding.

THE FIRST MESSAGES I RECEIVED from the cemetery were unsettling, scary even. *Have I lost it? Am I falling into the rabbit hole of grief? Going back to the days and weeks of weeping that left me exhausted, able to do little for myself? No, it's something else. Messages. For me. From them.*

Curiosity pulls me to the hill. Or it is a disturbance: a headstone rising or sinking without explanation or bare ground appearing where grass had grown, outlining the casket below. *I will go, spend time gardening, hear what they have to say.* So that becomes the weight of it.

TODAY I WONDER, THOUGH. *After Henry's death, why had it taken him fifteen years to show himself? The others, my aunts and parents, showed themselves to me not long after they died. Maybe it was the additional journey I feared he would have to make to pay for his stubbornness, his own unwillingness to make peace with his illness, his insistence that he would beat the odds. No one ever won that battle. Not even him.*

HE READ THE RESULTS of his routine blood tests, then spoke to me, his clear blue eyes fixed on the rows of numbers on the page, "They've got the wrong one, honey. Switched charts, don't you think?" His gut feeling, the barometer he had used all his life, was no longer accurate. A beehive invaded his gut, bouncing and buzzing off the walls of his insides, stinging him, distracting him so that he no longer believed in his own abilities. It sheared the edges of his confidence and left a toxic spill in his gut. "Guess my luck's run out," he said. His body collapsed on the chair at the head of the table, pages of blood work scattered across the kitchen floor.

He didn't do failure. Oh, he would allow small slivers of defeat to pierce his self-assurance in a casual moment as he and I walked along Chicago's lakefront. After humming a few bars of "Stars Fell on Alabama," he would pause and acknowledge a small battle he had lost at the office. That would be it. Defeat was given grudgingly.

He was six-foot-two, wore a size 46-long suit and filled every inch of his clothes. He began as a bicycle salesman at Morrie Mages and worked his way up into a partnership of a highly successful, small manufacturing plant. He hand-picked employees. He knew where every piece of stock was stored.

He had enough trust to defer to me, let me in. We had a friendship that worked. But in his mind, I know that he felt he had to pull at least two-thirds of the weight.

The confirmed diagnosis changed everything. He second-guessed every decision and looked over his shoulder more than he looked ahead. He hugged the boys more. Spent more time at home. I watched him disappear into his home office, sit at his desk, make notes on his calendar, call his business partner more often. The buzzing inside his gut continued to clamor for his attention, distracting him from the low-level humor that had been the background music in our kitchen for twenty-two years. He still wore his Mickey Mouse tie to executive meetings at the office, but I knew he no longer believed he was living in the Magic Kingdom, or in luck, grace, or good fortune.

I KNEW HE HAD GIVEN UP TRYING to broker a deal when he refused to join the boys and me at the dinner table, instead preferring to lie in his recliner in the darkened back room. He no longer invited his youngest son to crawl into his lap or asked the oldest about school. He was silent, withdrawn into himself, not even leaving the chair to sleep in our bed. That's when I feared that the part of him that was up for the fight had died. He knew he no longer could negotiate. There was no winning.

The rest of him took three weeks, three long weeks when he stopped speaking and became the other Henry. We were all angry about his withdrawal. It seemed cruel that he was closing the door on his life three weeks early. Three weeks less of the youngest son's childhood, of the older son's adolescence, of time with the four grown children and grandchildren from his first family, of time with me.

But what did I know of how one prepares for this kind of a journey? All I knew was that he was packing away a part of himself we loved, sealing it in a suitcase, outfitting himself for the journey. Then I remembered his favorite phrase when his friends asked for advice, always the same, "Go through the open door." Was this what he was doing?

After he died I found a scribble of numbers tallied on the front page of his personal calendar under the heading, "Net Worth." At first, this horrified me. He was so much more than that! But then, I really did understand. He boiled it down to what his death would offer in practical terms, the kind he understood.

My wish for him was for a kinder death at home surrounded by family, but he waited until he became too ill, and it was the hospital, not his family, that nursed him as he died. My youngest stepson and I shared much of the vigil, along with machines and tubes that beeped and dispensed medicine to prolong his life four more days.

I knew home was the only place where a man like him would say private goodbyes. I believed that home was where he would have told me what he had kept fastened close to his breastbone, those messages that flowed from blood and heart and body, messages held in a tightly sealed envelope only he could open. But doing that meant acknowledging he had lost the battle. Those conversations never happened.

I HAVE WAITED all these years to speak with him again.

As HE DIED HE SAID over and over, "I'm okay. I'm okay. I'm okay." He never spoke of making peace with his life or said any final words to anyone. He knew he was dying but would not name it except to say, "I'm okay." He could have asked for absolution, help, assistance. The only time in those four days he accepted help was the last time he struggled to stand. He allowed a nurse to hold his arm.

Not that the staff at the hospital weren't professional and compassionate. They were. It just wasn't his gig. Being in the hospital meant losing. He would disclose nothing from a hospital bed surrounded by nurses and aides. Strangers. Oh, he gave the world a wave of his hand, carefree and loose, but he wasn't that at all. He played it close and tight to the end.

THE DAY HE WAS BURIED was blustery, sunless, a bitter November day. My mood felt as gray as the slate steps that lined the walkway to the front porch. Wind whipped at the top of the hill and the small green canvas awning fluttered over the grave site at the highest point on our property. This place he had chosen himself.

Gravediggers had brought the backhoe the day before and dug the rectangular hole. They piled red clay in a mound next to it, covered it with artificial grass so the combination of red North Carolina clay and bright green grass made the cemetery look like some kind of garish, out-of-season Christmas decoration. By then I was mostly numb, had moments when I felt the loss intensely, then blurred back to numb. There had been all that stuff to do: obtaining death certificates and opening safe deposit boxes, as well as selecting the coffin, his burial clothes, the clothes I would wear, and the boys' outfits. I opened the refrigerator. I stood in front of the open door and wondered *who is it that lives on platters of lunch meat, cheese cut in cubes, bundt cakes? What ever happened to my vegetable bin full of lettuce, tomatoes, fresh fruit?*

Several days before the funeral I made an effort to grocery shop. I wandered through the produce department piling bunches of radishes into a plastic bag. I put them back on the pile when I remembered that Henry, who loved radishes, was dead, and had been for days. I left the store empty-handed.

The dog who slept next to my bed and had raced about happily sniffing freshly dug earth as the men dug the grave now refused to leave his bed. "Come on, Brown Dog," I whistled and cajoled, but the stray we had adopted nearly a year ago would not budge. He lay head down, paws splayed in front of him, and did not leave the bed until the funeral was over and the hearse drove away. Brown Dog died two months later of the same disease as Henry.

The navy dress I chose I never wore again. It felt too heavy, the weight of it woven with sorrow. I walked with the others to the top of the hill.

I recall the weather mostly, how gray the clouds were, sunless and dark, how cold the wind felt on my face, how my back hurt from crying so much, how everything seemed to move both in slow motion and a rapid blur at the same time. I do remember receiving a rectangular flag, an American flag that had been folded, and looking down at my hands, seeing it and thinking *I didn't realize a folded flag was so heavy*, wondering why I had been given a flag, then, *yes, he was in the Navy*. I looked at the others seated on chairs provided by the funeral home: family members, our two children, my stepchildren and step-grandchildren, and friends who came from Chicago. Everyone was so still and silent. They looked like cardboard cut-outs of themselves placed on the top of the hill. The chairs were metal. *Cold. Cold as the November red clay at my feet.*

We were all suddenly back at the house pulling out platters of food, sitting in the living room where a corner was crowded with baskets of peace lilies. I assumed some well-meaning person brought them back to the house after the service. I couldn't recall if anyone asked me, my brain was in such a fog. *Peace?* I felt little of the comfort the flower's name offered. A large, multicolor arrangement called "The Eternal Garden Basket" sat next to a raised stand displaying a massive heart of blood-red roses draped with a purple banner reading "Forever Missing You." *My living room is a funeral parlor all over again. The scent of flowers is too sweet, cloying. I love flowers, but* this. *These arrangements are so unnatural. What I feel is so present.* I wondered if I would ever feel comfort and peace in my home again.

Now that it was done, the business we humans made to fill the void of loss left a silent restlessness in the air. I knew that my stepchildren and step-grandchildren would leave soon. They had spent close to a week at the house holding each other together, helping me. And they had done a remarkable job of coming from all corners of the country to help cook and clean and do the driving and say goodbye to their father.

Without thinking, I rose from my chair and left the room. I returned moments later. I handed my oldest stepdaughter the wide gold band I had removed from Henry's left hand at the hospital. "I want you to have his wedding ring. Save it for one of your boys for his wedding." I gave the oldest son the blanket that Henry used to cover his legs when he was chilled. He will spread it across his own legs on the long plane trip back to California. I handed the youngest son an oil painting of a seascape that Henry's uncle painted. I offered the youngest daughter his Mickey Mouse watch.

So it was done. Henry was the first to be buried at the top of the windswept hill. At the time, the land was as barren as my feelings. There were no shrubs, no garden gate or grave markers or stone bench or crape myrtle. But that spring he was close, accessible, and I visited with him as I grieved, planted grass seed over the rectangle of red clay that marked his grave, and ordered that first flat brass marker for Sweet Woods Garden.

TODAY HE HAS RETURNED and I want to have that final conversation. He walks close to me, carrying his confidence to me, bringing his message like a gift in his hands. *"Here. Take my beliefs, my confidence. I cannot use these things where I am now. I see your path and all your careful, plodding efforts to set the boys on their voyage and to make a solid life for yourself."* He stands facing me, places both his hands on my shoulders. That familiar tingle ripples through my body. He looks down and grins, *"You worry too long, too often about outcomes. Here."* He takes one of my hands between his two hands, *"Take the energy, the passion for the life I have lived and use it now in yours. Your path is forged with grief and a history of long love. Use that energy to go through the open door. Teach our children to do that, too."*

I feel the warmth of his lips on my cheek. As I lean forward to touch him, his image fades. *Nothing vanishes. Nothing.*

TODAY IS A WATERCOLOR WASH. Rain has fallen all week pulling down russet, gold and burnt-umber leaves. They lie knee-deep at the base of the gnarled beech trees in the front yard. With this November rain, nearly all the leaves on the property will be down. The last green, save the pines and the balsam fir beyond Sweet Woods Garden, will vanish until April buds begin to swell. A family of red-breasted nuthatches flies in and out of the tiny red-roof birdhouse that hangs from the crape myrtle tree in the perennial bed at the top of the hill. They will over-winter here. My lab, JB, the shelter puppy that joined us after Brown Dog died, is watching the birds intently, mindful they are beyond his boundaries but hopeful they will trespass into his. His eye travels to a pair of white squirrels that have slipped from their nest in a tall pine tree at the back of the property and scamper through the grass to forage beneath the trees in the front yard for beech nuts that have fallen. These squirrels, unique to this area, stand out, their white coats like snow against the carpet of leaves. My puppy chases them. They race for safety high in the trees.

Sage, rosemary, lemon thyme and flat-leaf parsley will keep green at the elevation of my house and become perennial herbs. I planted them in the garden just at the edge of the house, steps away from the kitchen and handy for cooking. I will use them for Thanksgiving, Christmas and daily for soups and stews.

The grounds will soon become stark and barren, and I might feel inclined toward melancholy unless I understand that this is a time for rest in the garden in preparation for a huge release of energy to come. Winter is a time when color turns drab as plants prepare for the burst of energy required for spring bloom-ing. Leaves drop and surface flowers decay, providing food neces-sary for rebirth, not unlike the days after human dying when the body is in transition, shedding its old self, preparing, giving way to the spirit.

Joe-Pye weed stands nearly nine-feet high below Sweet Woods Garden, adding a border of purple stems, serrated leaves and rose-colored clusters of flowers. This plant often continues to bloom after everything else has faded. What I first thought to be a pesky weed, natives here taught me is a perennial herb used to relieve kidney and urinary tract discomfort and is drunk as a tea to break a high fever. I consider it good luck and let it grow and spread.

Joining my yellow lab, I kick the leaves at my feet and upturn tiny insects. They crave spaces that are damp and still, places where there is no light; places that smell of decay; places that break down to feed new growth, like nurse trees in old forests, their decaying wood feeding seedlings that spring up in the corpse of a fallen great tree. Grubs will burrow in the earth beneath the grass and emerge as beetles in the spring. A lone cricket jumps from a tiny twig among the leaves. Flower roots suck chlorophyll from plant leaves, leaching the last light energy and storing it for growth next spring.

These spaces that are dark and damp call me to look beyond what is on the surface of my life at what is floating, visible, easy to see. I am learning to be still, watch for the unseen, look for the significant in the familiar, find simple truths in everyday life. All the shifts of the seasons are right here at my feet in the life cycle of a tiny cricket and in those spaces – dark, damp, and still.

I was pregnant for the fourth time and I hoped, after three failed pregnancies, that I was not going to miscarry *this* time. I had managed to get through that milestone fifth month and my doctor assured me that my placenta was taking over and producing hormones. I no longer had to live with low levels of progesterone and estrogen in my unreliable body, a body that disappointed, was *Not Enough*. I finally began to believe *Baby*. For the first time in my life my skin glowed as my body pumped out a choreography of luteinizing and follicle-stimulating hormones, all in the right balance.

Mom and Dad visited and fussed over my ever-expanding stomach, made plans for a baby shower, cautioned me about the changes a baby would make in our lives. Mom leaned forward as we sat together, the two of us enjoying a private moment, as she reminisced about my birth.

I was born in a Catholic hospital, the Coleman Hospital for Women, in Indianapolis. The nurses were nuns. Mom said she was given an injection, twilight sleep. When she woke up, there I was. "That's just the way many births were handled in the 1940s," she said. Then the day after I was born, nuns came into Mom's room and told her she didn't have enough milk, bound her breasts and bottle fed me. My mother put it this way, "I wasn't able to nurse you." She looked at the floor as she spoke.

I did not question her, even though I had so many questions for my mother, who had shared so little of how she felt about anything, much less motherhood. I was hungry for information, but I kept still, afraid that her sudden revelation would be her last. Was her inability to breast feed due to what her diet lacked during the war years? Was she intimidated by the hospital nuns? Surely her mother had nursed all of her children. Maybe they had never spoken about sex, babies, marriage. Any of it.

Formula was fashionable at the time I was born. It was homemade, created from a combination of Karo syrup and water. I found the recipe my mother was given at the hospital dutifully copied into my baby book.

What had happened? She lifted her head. Her answer was vague. She was uneasy sharing reasons for her failure, but clear about letting me know breast feeding had been difficult for her. Her telling me this mattered. A lot. Maybe I was hung up on being a natural mother, providing a different sort of parenting than she had given me.

It was unsettling. How remarkable that she told me she couldn't nurse at this moment, when I finally was pregnant after years of infertility. Infertility had robbed me of my confidence, my sense of adequacy as a woman, and left my self esteem eroded, fragile.

Pregnant . . . loss of child.

Pregnant . . . loss.

Pregnant . . . loss.

Like a mantra I never wanted to learn.

I remember my paternal grandmother and my Italian aunts huddled together in a circle on Sundays, rosaries working overtime, praying the beads for a pregnant sister, asking Mary to protect the baby from *malocchio*, the evil eye. *They nursed everywhere, at weddings, funerals, and at home with confidence.* I remember one of the first weddings I attended as a young child, staring in horror at my aunts sitting (dressed to the nines in their finest), all nursing. I had never seen exposed breasts before. I was embarrassed and wondered why no one else seemed upset.

At the time, I did not see that, in disclosing this secret, my mother, such a private woman, was sharing an intimate part of her past. It was like taking a huge step outside her carefully constructed world. She had offered something she rarely gave, her candor, her openness, her doubt. Today I understand that she offered that part of herself, but then I was younger, full of my own doubts and hormones, and needing her mothering.

Somehow, hearing my mother's uncertainty about her ability to do such a natural thing left me anxious. I remember lying in my hospital bed after my first son, John, was born and looking at my beautiful baby, my perfect baby, being so completely in love, not being able to take my eyes off him, marveling that my husband and I had made this beautiful, blond child and feeling misgivings about having *Enough* milk.

Breast feeding was popular in the 1980s. La Leche League was available. The nurses at Michael Reese Hospital, where I delivered, encouraged it. Everyone was patient, yet I kept hearing my mother's voice, *"Not Enough milk. Not Enough. Not Enough."* I knew my parents had long-term sexual problems. This might have been a part of it, but still I believe knowing this, having this simple knowledge at a time when I was terribly vulnerable, was very powerful for me.

WE TOOK JOHN HOME and I nursed him. He weighed nearly nine pounds at birth. I was worried. Did I have *Enough* milk to feed such a big baby? All his development was on track. It was all okay at first. Then, he didn't gain weight as rapidly as the developmental charts suggested, my pediatrician stated. I heard the voice: *Not Enough, Not Enough.* Except for weighing on the low end of the charts, he continued to develop normally. I did not want to give up nursing and continued until he was four months old. At my pediatrician's urging I began giving him formula.

At five months of age he began to have absence seizures which lasted until he was eighteen months of age and disappeared as mysteriously as they began. That was when he was diagnosed with a developmental delay. "Etiology unknown," the pediatric neurologist whom I consulted told me when I asked him the cause. He could find nothing in John's history or mine to explain it. Nothing that happened during the pregnancy, nothing that happened during his birth. His Apgars at birth were all nines, a near-perfect nine out of ten. His development until five months was on target. I reviewed every moment of my pregnancy, every decision I had made during those nine months, but never found an explanation for it. Henry had four children with his former wife. None of them had this history. *My genes. Not Enough.*

All I could remember was my mother saying, "I didn't have enough milk for you." *Not Enough. Not Enough.* This legacy passed on to me. Can one be poisoned by emotion? By something not so clearly stated as displeasure, resentment, or fault finding? By something subtle and said at a time when I must have been wide open, susceptible, insecure? I reran each day of my pregnancy: where I traveled, what I ate, what I might have *breathed in.* Maybe I shouldn't have gone swimming at the Y where the water was treated. Did I use cleaning products that were too strong? What about automobile exhaust in all those traffic jams in Chicago? Was it the anesthesia in the delivery room? The fertility drugs?

I looped around in endless circles of guilt until the pediatric neurologist said after so many return appointments, "We'll never know the cause. You did nothing wrong. Lots of kids have seizures that disappear eventually. Many adults function normally unaware they are having slight seizures. Stop beating yourself up about this. Enjoy your son. Many kids outgrow this as their brain matures." So I tried to follow his advice, but the memory of giving up nursing haunted me, and I continued an insane review of every movement I had made when I was pregnant, everything I had put into my body.

MY INFERTILITY HAD STRIPPED both me and Henry bare. Getting pregnant had become some sort of a scientific experiment involving measuring my temperature on a daily basis and orchestrating our sex life around the numbers on a thermometer, instead of paying attention to the pheromones that attracted us. Before that I had felt pretty, attractive, and loved dressing in lace, wearing ruffles and lots of makeup. But now I was obsessed with the goal, getting it right, taking my temperature, stripped down to tee shirts and jeans. My body never seemed good enough.

After months of trying, I did get pregnant and walked around on tiptoes afraid to disturb the developing egg. Then, a bit of spotting. "Nothing to worry about. It happens often early in a pregnancy," my infertility specialist said. Next, big, ugly clots of bright red blood, the baby passing from me, leaving my body as if the habitat were too toxic. I felt ugly, barren, inadequate, and looked at my husband who had borne this process with me because he loved me and wanted to have a second family. He held his hands, palms up, and shrugged, "I love you, babe."

I could hear my mother's voice, the echo of *Not Enoughs*, and I thought maybe there was not enough *me* to do this. I was missing that special ingredient that's necessary for motherhood and I didn't know what it was. I didn't know how to get it, and I couldn't ask my mother because she had told me she had never been *Enough*.

I strolled in the park with my pregnant friends, their big baby bellies pushing out the fronts of their shirts. They told me, "Just relax. Take it easy. Everything will be fine." I wanted to scream and find fault with these rosy-cheeked friends.

I was feeling murderous toward my health insurance company when a letter arrived informing me they would not pay for further infertility treatments, because infertility was not, in 1976, considered a medical condition. Well then, what is it? A defect in character? I asked a friend who was an attorney to send a letter to the insurance company to reconsider their decision. I suffered the indignity and embarrassment of having to tell him, in detail, of my failure at parenthood.

JOHN WAS A DELIGHT despite his developmental struggles. When Henry wasn't at work, he and John traveled all over the city of Chicago to the Fannie Mae seconds store, two blocks from his manufacturing plant, and to Lou Mitchell's restaurant for breakfast on Saturdays. Lou Mitchell handed them each his signature box of Milk Duds on the way out the door. They drove to ethnic neighborhoods for blood sausage and seeded rye bread when Henry's Danish-German father visited. At fifty-two, Henry was a committed dad who wanted to spend as much time as possible with his son. John fit right into our lifestyle. We pulled his high chair up to the dining room table when we had an adult dinner party.

WHEN I WAS THIRTY-NINE, I knew that if I wanted another child I would have to return to the fertility specialist. Truth is, in spite of how difficult it was for us to have children, I wanted to try again. I had fleeting thoughts while I was pregnant: *Are you crazy to do this again?* Then I looked at John playing with a best friend in a playgroup. I watched John's delight planting a single seed of corn and watching it grow, "Look, Mom! The corn seed is a green plant now!" I saw the pleasure in his face, felt the hum in my belly, and looked at Henry and thought, *It's all okay.*

After another miscarriage at forty-one, Jason was born in the same hospital suite with the same surgeon performing a second (elected that time because I was so high-risk) rapid surgical delivery without hours of labor. The only surprise was that, as big and blond as John was at birth, Jason was a short, chubby baby with a head full of black hair. I felt I was *Enough.*

Henry brought John to the hospital to peek through the glass window of the nursery, holding him high in his arms to see his brother, "I ordered a sister. Send him back," John exclaimed. Henry and I roared with laughter. Jiggling from the laughter made my incision hurt, but I felt complete. *We were a family unit.*

Jason was an easy baby until three weeks of age when he developed the longest-running case of colic in the history of my pediatrician's practice. His sensitive stomach refused everything *but* breast milk. I nursed him successfully until he was ten months old. We all hummed along in a cocoon of domesticity, our cups overflowing with comfort and stability.

The kitchen became my favorite place in the house. That was where we all greeted Dad after work as he tumbled into the house, tie askew, his white shirt-sleeves rolled to the elbows, frazzled from managing his office staff, the manufacturing plant, Chicago traffic. That was where I prepared a million home-cooked meals: roast chicken, pot roast, meatloaf, fat blueberry muffins studded with so many blueberries the kids' teeth were blue, spaghetti and meatballs (my grandmother's recipe made with beef and finely ground veal), and fried zucchini blossoms from the backyard garden. And why not? I spent my childhood in my mother's kitchen.

From the time I was nine years old (then it wasn't considered dangerous to leave a child alone with the oven on), I mixed and baked cookies after Sunday school while my parents were at church. I would set the cookies, soft, fragrant, and hot from the oven on cooling racks on the dining room table. The scent emanating from the oven pulled my younger brother, Paul, from his Lincoln Logs, to steal a few cookies. When my parents returned, we would all climb into Dad's Chevy to drive the twenty-five minutes to the Kensington area on Chicago's south side to have dinner with Grandma and my eighteen cousins and nine aunts and uncles, thirty-four noisy Italians at

the house on Normal Avenue eating a homemade meal, recon-
necting with each other around the table.

Kitchen. La cucina was home for me. Kitchen was comfort.

Bounty. *Plenty.* I basked in the glow of *our* family. I was
immersed in marriage and motherhood, busy with pre-school,
kindergarten, tee-ball practice, arranging our basement into a
giant playroom for birthday parties, Cub Scout meetings and
roller skating across the smooth cement floor during the bitter,
snowy Chicago winters.

The truth is: having children made me feel I was *Enough.*
Balanced. Balanced like the food on the dinner plates on our
kitchen table: circles of protein, vegetables, starch. The word
family rang in my ears like a small silver bell softly tinkling in
the back of my mind. *Oneness. Congruity. Identity.* The words
Not Enough dimmed as I became a successful mom, a parent
who I knew someday would be called "the old lady," my kids
worrying over me as surely as I was fussing over them. I prayed
the *Not Enough* legacy would not pass to them.

These were such solid years until Henry was diagnosed.
These years created a foundation which enabled me to survive
the next ten rocky years.

My throat was dry, scratchy. I regretted having declined
that second glass of iced tea at lunch, but it was not
thirst. Surely, it was hot. It was August in Arkansas and my
long brown hair felt damp at the base of my neck in spite of the
short distance I walked from the dining room of the complex
to the building next door. Stress. That was it. What did it matter, my thirst? I would not quench it here.

Goose bumps rose on my arms as I pushed open the glass doors to the climate-controlled environment of Parkway Village Care Center. I rode an empty elevator, grateful that no one was in the car. I let out a long sigh, dropped my shoulders, and closed my eyes as the elevator shuddered and rose. The doors opened onto the second floor to the smell of Pine Sol and freshly waxed linoleum. Patients clustered around a circular nursing station just ahead of me. A few sat in wheelchairs, immobilized by medications or disease, or both. Many paced, urgently tracing and retracing the same movements. One woman walked briskly, arms swinging, as she rounded the perimeter of the room. She turned her head from side-to-side as if looking for something. I watched as the woman stopped and nodded to the nurse at the nursing station. The nurse acknowledged her by raising her eyebrows slightly, then picked up a telephone. The woman resumed her patrol of the room's perimeter.

I REMEMBERED THE LAST TIME I visited Mom with my brother, Paul. "She's different than last time." I placed my hand on his arm as I spoke to him.

"Right." His shoulders hunched forward as if he was making himself ready. Mom, dressed in a sloppy sweat suit, walked past without acknowledging either of us. Our mother who had always dressed immaculately in hand-made, tailored clothes, her heart and ears ever open to us. Paul turned and followed this silent woman.

"Go ahead. Walk along with her. Come up from the side, though. You might startle her if you come from behind. She is liable to . . . well . . . hit you . . . strike out."

34

"No. You're kidding," he laughed softly. "Mom? Our Mom?"

I knew he didn't get it. Not because he didn't understand. He didn't want to understand. He was the assistant fire chief in the small Texas town where he lived, rode in the ambulances as a paramedic and kept an emergency medical kit under the driver's seat of his van. I watched him handle people at an accident scene once. He was professional, competent, confident. But this wasn't a stranger. This was *his mother.*

I nodded and moved to the other side of the room.

My brother approached her carefully. "Hi, Maribel." The wizened woman turned toward him. I watched the shock register on my brother's face. How the disease had stolen her beauty, aged her pretty face, leaving it a river of wrinkles, and turned her skin the color of putty. She had not seen the sun in months. Her body was a pharmacy of chemicals.

"Why, Bill!" Suddenly, she was animated. Maribel turned to Paul, grinned, slid close to him, slipped her arm through his, "Let's go to my room, eh? How about it?" Paul flushed, embarrassed by her open flirtation. How tangled her connections were! She was back in her hometown, seventeen years old, and with Bill, her first boyfriend.

Well, at least she is happy, smiling. Hope Paul can handle this.

She pulled at Paul's arm, tugging him, now laughing.

"Maribel, I just can't go with you right this moment. I've . . . I've got an appointment." My brother stepped back a few feet. She looked away from my brother, ran one hand up and down her arm, and returned to her pacing, her eyes expressionless, veiled by illness.

Paul walked to the nursing station and shared a quiet conversation with the staff.

I stepped around a wheelchair to sign the visitors' register before sitting on the narrow, backless bench in the alcove next to the nursing station. Each visit I had sat there, needing moments to gather myself before visiting Mom. The bench, upholstered with floral fabric in shades of peach and pale green, reminded me of the dressing table in Mom and Dad's bedroom where we had shared so many confidences and passages.

THE POST-WORLD WAR II brick bungalow was tiny. The rooms were small and close together, so close that a voice could easily carry from one end of the house to the other. I stepped into my parents' bedroom.

"Mom, can I borrow your pearl choker for the party this weekend?" I had already placed my hands on the knobs of the cherry dresser knowing what the answer would be.

"Yes, dear," Mom answered from the kitchen, "Look in the first drawer of my dresser, top right." The dresser was part of a set purchased when they were newlyweds in 1927, with a double bed with a cherry head- and foot-board, a vanity with a round mirror framed in matching cherry and a covered bench. Traditional in design, the wood was a highly finished, rich, red brown. Mom polished the set every week.

Behind me, the wood Venetian blinds in the casement window were pulled up all the way. Afternoon sunlight spilled into the room and danced off the cuff links in Dad's jewelry tray on the top of the dresser.

It seemed odd this time, being in the bedroom with permission. Often I would sneak in just to explore in the drawers. Unsanctioned visits into their bedroom were made to find that part of them that would fill in the blanks, explain who they really were, what secrets they had. I grasped the knob and pulled out the drawer. The bottom was lined from end to end with green felt, the edges meticulously clipped with Mom's pinking shears. Those pinking shears were used everywhere in the house to be sure there were no loose ends anywhere. Arranged in a single layer across the felt in groupings were bracelets, matching earrings, necklaces and pins. *Tidy. Neat. Mom's life. No secrets here.*

I lifted the pearls from the drawer and held them to my cheek, feeling their coolness. They smelled faintly of Joy perfume. I put the pearls around my neck, attached the rhinestone daisy clasp through a slide. At the mirror I saw the reflection of a young woman, shorter than her peers, shoulder-length hair, deep-set eyes and a heart-shaped face. At this distance from the mirror, the braces on my teeth and breakouts on my forehead didn't seem as noticeable as they did when I examined them up close every night in the bathroom mirror.

The pearls were the sort of jewelry Mom wore to "set off" an outfit, as she described it. I wanted to look perfect in my purple mohair sweater for the dance that weekend. How hard I had worked to get rid of the chubby girl who seemed not to want to leave my body. How I had loved being able to shop in a store that carried regular sizes instead of Mom buying patterns, fabric and making clothes for me because I was such an obese child.

HOW MY IMAGE OF MYSELF had changed! Or was I still struggling with the ghosts of those early childhood memories?

ME: SHY, OBESE, always wanting to hide behind my mother's skirt, a book, a drawing. Me? Dance? In public? In front of an audience? On stage? The pink satin ballet slippers I held in my hands had long, shiny ribbons that wrapped up the leg and promised grace and beauty. The toes were squared at the end to hold a wooden peg. That was where the dancer (me) was supposed to balance the entire weight of her gawky body. Somehow holding the slippers by their gossamer satin ribbons led me to believe that once they were on my feet I would be transformed from a withdrawn, graceless child to a swan.

The two of us, Mom and me, had gone to the Civic Opera House in Chicago to see the ballet *Swan Lake*. I gazed mesmerized by the beauty and grace of the ballerinas moving across the stage, their lithe bodies floating in what seemed like effortless rhythm to the sound of the orchestra. I was transfixed. Mom sat next to me in her favorite Sunday pillbox hat and a tailored coat she usually reserved for Reverend Shuler's Sunday sermons or her League of Women Voters' meetings. I sat next to her, feeling grown up, ready to become graceful, elegant. Watching *Swan Lake* convinced me that I would become what I was seeing. In the ballet, the princess is turned into a swan by an evil curse, then is redeemed by a prince. The story was better than any sermon I had heard Reverend Schuler preach and much, much, more glamorous.

The performance and the lunch afterward at Marshall Field's led to a discussion about taking ballet lessons. Me? Dance? I was embarrassed by my weight and didn't want to exercise. I hated going to the gym on Fridays because I could not hide in the one-piece, blue bloomer uniforms we were required to wear. At that time there were almost no organized sports for girls. My sole foray into the world of the physical was the fourth-grade girls' baseball team.

I played one game. I was the last picked for a team. My first time up to bat, the ball flew past me. "Strike one!" My head snapped. I never even saw the ball. I'd never played like this before, for real. I had always got a second chance. "Try again, dear," then praised for the effort. "Strike two!" The same. "Strike three. Out." Humiliation in front of my peers felt awful. I ran from the field, sped the seven blocks home from the Roosevelt School playground and never played again.

But ballet, now that seemed gentle, refined, more my speed. Off I went to ballet school. I liked to practice. No, I *loved* to practice. In practice, I could make mistakes with the teacher gently correcting me. No three strikes there. What I did not understand was that after all those practice sessions, first position, second position, third, fourth and fifth, there would be a very public recital on a stage.

Mom was thrilled to be one of the mothers sewing the bluebird costume, a fitted bodice with a matching electric-blue, net tutu skirt, and a blue skull cap with a bright yellow beak. It made me look like a sort of Big Bird gone down the rabbit hole in *Alice in Wonderland*. After countless hours of fittings and rehearsals, the night of the performance arrived. I had practiced for hours in the basement at home. The costume fit, and I had finally learned how to balance my amazing bulk and stand on my toes.

I was confident. *Prepared.*

I entered the stage and gazed past the floodlights into rows and rows of adults staring back at me. The teacher put on the familiar music and signaled for us to begin. The other two bluebirds began their graceful dance. My mind went blank.

I stood frozen in place. The other two girls dance flawlessly. I glanced offstage at my teacher who was wild-eyed, frantically waving at me, her lips mouthing, "Go! Move!"

I tried copying the other girls' movements, but that strategy left me about three beats behind them. I wasn't graceful. I was comedic. Instead of blending in, instead of being part of an elegant trio, I stuck out. *Again*. With each beat of the music I became more and more self-conscious, more confused. Laughter, not applause, floated up on stage. *More laughter.*

"Oh. I see you found them."

"I'll be careful with these, Mom."

"Of course you will, dear." She looked into the drawer as she spoke, her hand meticulously straightening and rearranging the jewelry I had moved a fraction of an inch when I had pulled out the pearls. Mom's hands caressed the pearls. I knew many of the pieces were gifts from Dad.

"There's nothing like wearing a good piece of jewelry to make you feel as if you are dressed and ready for anything. Let's try those pearls on and see how they look on you."

I removed my pastel-colored pop-it beads and watched Mom fasten the clasp around my neck.

"There, now! Oh, my, you look . . . lovely. Older." Mom's hand went to her heart.

"I do? Great!"

I sat on the bench basking in my mother's praise, feeling nearly pretty and something else I had not felt before. I felt something like *belonging*. I envisioned joining my aunts as they shared confidences on Sundays at Grandma's.

Mom opened the second drawer of her vanity, reached to the back, and drew out a small, black velvet box. She opened it and stared at it a long time, then handed a ring to me.

"This is a special piece and, although I no longer wear it, I want you to see it since you are at the age to appreciate these things." The oval, green jade ring was set in sterling silver. Oriental lettering circled the band.

"You don't wear this? Why? It's gorgeous!"

"Your father didn't give it to me." Her face darkened. "It was a gift from Yoshi, a Japanese man, someone I met before your father." Mom's carefully constructed image collapsed as her shoulders slumped and she let out a long, deep breath. My mother, this careful woman whose pinking-shears kept all the ends neatly clipped, was unraveling.

"Oh? A boyfriend you had before Dad? Wow! Was he handsome? Did you go out for dinner? Dancing? Did you ever wear a kimono?

"No, no," she laughed, "but I did learn about Japanese food and we did have dinner together."

"Tell me more."

Mom looked up at the open door, stood, walked over to it, and closed it. "He was a Japanese businessman I met at the office where I was working as a secretary. He came to America on an extended business trip from Japan and lived in the United States for over a year." I waited through a long pause for her to continue the story.

Mom pointed to the dresser. "This dresser is old. We bought it, your father and me, just after we got married. It was such a huge sacrifice in the thirties." I watched with surprise as Mom, seemingly lost in memory, began to open her closed life.

"But what about Yoshi?" I was eager for more.

"We started dating, and we really liked each other, but his family was traditional Japanese and never would have approved of our marrying. So, we couldn't continue." Mom stared at the ring in my palm. "Before he returned to Japan, he gave me this ring. He said it was a token of our friendship."

Stunned by this new image of my mother, I was not sure what to say. Just when I opened my mouth to speak, she stepped away from me and her past.

"Well! Enough of this daydreaming. I've got a meal to think about." She backed away from the mirror and slipped her hands into her apron pockets. Then she stood a moment as if thinking about something.

"Put it on. See if it fits. Someday this ring will be yours."

I slid the jade ring on my finger. It fit perfectly. I held up my hand in the light and admired the ring, "Mom, I don't know what to say. This is the most beautiful thing I've ever seen. And to think some day it will be mine."

Mom leaned forward and whispered in my ear, "I wouldn't have it any other way. You are my only daughter. It should be yours." She kissed my cheek. "But, let this be our secret. You father might not be pleased to revisit this memory."

"Sure, Mom. Sure."

Mom took both hands from her apron pockets and placed them on my shoulders. I felt her hands press into them firmly. "And, know this. Hold out for the man you love. No matter what."

I RAN MY HANDS across the padded fabric of the bench, pushed back my headband, and tucked my shirt into my slacks. I would be groomed and pulled together to honor what had been.

Mom walked alone past me. Her hair had been clipped into a short, mannish cut. Even though I had suggested this haircut to simplify grooming and bathing, she looked less familiar without the frame of soft curls around her face. She wore the formless sweat suit I had purchased on my last visit six weeks ago. *I know these practical clothes are right for her illness and abilities*, said the self-talk that rambled in my brain as I swallowed the tears that swelled in my dry throat. I watched my petite, style-conscious mother disappear beneath bulky layers of cheap fleece. Today her feet flip-flopped along the floor in a pair of too-large, pink house slippers that I do not recognize. I remember the story Mom told me about feet just after she graduated second in her high school class.

"LOOK AT ME! Look at me *hard. Now.*" Grandma Belle, Mom's mother, stood face-to-face with her daughter in the hallway of their farmhouse in southern Illinois. "Is this the life you want? Canning and cleaning and cooking, Maribel?"

Mom told me she was stunned because her mother rarely spoke to her in this way, almost never raising her voice. She told me that her mother bent down and removed her serviceable work shoes, one of the two pairs she owned, not counting the high rubber boots she wore in the garden.

"Look at my feet! That's what you'll have if you stay."

Mom said she could never remember seeing her mother barefoot. She looked at her mother's swollen feet, her toes buckled and turned on each other. Bumps protruded from the outside of the big toe near the instep. The skin was red, rough and calloused.

"'That's eight babies all too close together, standing over the stove, hanging clothes outside to dry, *running*, running to keep up all day long." She slid her shoes back on her feet. "Used to have a tiny foot like you. Size five-and-a-half narrow, trim, so trim it fit right into the palm of your Dad's hand."

Mom said that hearing this intimate information about her parents made her blush.

"Now I'm two sizes bigger with flat feet that hurt all the time just like my back, just like other things you don't know about."

Mom said she felt her eyes fill with tears, but somehow she could not cry because of what else her mother said: "*Go!* Go to the Twin Cities. Get a job, a *desk* job. Work with your *mind*, not your body. Find a husband who can care for you so you can paint those pretty pictures you love."

In a further uncommon gesture, she kissed her daughter on the cheek before she returned to the kitchen.

Mom was gaunt. She flip-flopped past me without acknowledgment. I rose and followed the thin, shrunken ghost of a woman.

"Hello, Maribel. How are you today?" I walked beside Mom and addressed her by the only name she was likely to recognize. I knew she didn't remember being anyone's mother. She stopped moving, turned and looked at me with vacant eyes.

I gestured toward the alcove and the bench. "Let's sit and visit a moment. Here's a good spot."

I sat on the bench. Mom backed up to the bench and sat down, her body leaning slightly forward as if prepared to jump up at any moment. Her hands grasped her kneecaps as she stared straight ahead. I eased myself gently next to her so as not to startle her. I spoke slowly, struggling to stitch threads of memory into the gnarled mass that was her mind. Each visit I repeated the same names and anecdotes, hoping to find a key word, the one phrase that would connect us once again.

"Remember your son, Paul? How busy he was as a child waking up each day with his feet already moving even before they hit the floor? Your sewing room and the black Singer sewing machine? All those clothes you made for Paul and me? I never had to buy clothes until I left home. The times I came home from school and you had a cup of Lipton tea before starting dinner?"

I turned and faced her. *Nothing.* I looked down at my feet, then back at her. *There has got to be a key word, a phrase!*

I kept going.

"What about Dad? Your husband, John? All those Sundays we rode in the red and white Chevy to visit his family at the house on Normal Avenue? Mimi? Elna?"

A flicker.

She turned her head toward me, then away, and her vacant stare returned.

"What about the fluffy tapioca pudding you used to make with three extra egg whites? It looked like a white cloud floating in the blue bowl in the Frigidaire."

Nothing.

I kept at it, listing memories faster and faster as if the speed of the list might jar a memory loose: "The black iron skillet, homemade doughnuts, Swiss steak, pot roast, peanut butter cookies, cherry pie with cherries picked from Mrs. Reed's cherry tree next door." As I spoke, I slipped my arm slowly around Mom's shoulder and felt her bony shoulder blades press against my arm.

"MARIBEL, GET OUT BACK and help your father get those apples into the bushel baskets now before it rains. And take your sister Lorraine with you. Keep her out of my hair for a spell. Keep her little hands doing something useful. I've got twelve quarts of tomatoes to put up."

This was the business of Mom's life. The stories she told me helped me understand how much energy it took for her parents to manage the white, wood-frame farmhouse that her father built with a quarter-acre garden on the lot next door. Eighty years later, the house still stands on the corner at the crossroads in downtown Viola, population 800 then, 950 now. Some things never change.

People who lived with the seasons did not have time for much but church and family and their land. It was about keeping up and living in harmony with the seasons. As a child my mother's parents taught her the value of harmony, that life was about learning how to sustain that harmony by cooking a good stew, stirring the blend of hearty beef and root vegetables, simmering it to make food that stayed with you, kept you going.

Life was all about balance. Life was about doing the dance in the right rhythm so that the crab apples got harvested and made into jelly before the birds ate them or they rotted on the ground. Filling the root cellar with potatoes and turnips and parsnips so there were the makings for winter meals when the snow was heavy and deep, covering sleeping gardens.

It was about keeping the Christian balance that the Methodist minister preached every Sunday in the little white church (visible above the hollyhocks growing against the back fence) where Grandma played the organ: "Blessed Assurance, Jesus is Mine", "What a Friend We Have in Jesus", "The Old Rugged Cross." Work, pray, sleep, care for your family, harvest.

The early years of Mom's marriage had taught her the perils of discord and what it cost. The jarring noises early in her marriage (that I only discovered after she died by reading the few letters she left at the bottom of a drawer that implied a separation initiated by my mother early in their marriage) left her feeling out of place and sent her to her parents. Her parents saw the visit as improper, incorrect. *Unsuitable.* Even though Mom explained the circumstances carefully so that they knew she was in the right, *she was wrong.* She wasn't living in harmony with what was.

Not much room for dreams about becoming an artist and learning how to use that box of watercolors. Painting all the beauty that surrounded them: the streams with overhanging poplars, rustling in the wind, plowed fields, and fields of corn with tall, green stalks topped with yellow tassels blowing in the breeze like wisps of hair escaping from a young girl's ponytail.

I look around me in my own home at all the paintings my mother left, the pastoral scenes painted just blocks from her family home: cows grazing in fields of summer grasses with a bubbling stream in the background, a figure of a young boy sitting at the edge of a pond at dusk (taken from a photograph of Paul on a family vacation in Wisconsin), a winter scene of a cabin covered with billowy snow, all in shades of whites and grays. Mom might not have spoken her feelings. *She painted them.*

My mother said she harvested every kind of berry – gooseberry, raspberry, blackberry, huckleberry, blueberry, strawberry – until her hands bled the colors of summer. Her mother couldn't chastise her for her stained fingers that came from work, not from her painting. "You do that fancy artwork after your chores, young lady." Half-painted barns and fields full of autumn's blaze, greens and golds and reds, would have to wait until she harvested the last of the cabbages and put them in the side-yard root cellar, pulling open the door and stepping down the wood steps onto the bare earth floor smelling of Illinois' black dirt.

Sometimes my mother would eye the tire swing on the lowest branch of the apple tree ten feet away and swing on it on Sundays when Uncle Howard, her mother's brother, came to call. That's the day her mother rested. Her mother sat in church, then sat in a straight-backed chair in the back yard with Howard as they talked in low voices about family matters.

Grandpa disappeared on Sunday afternoons into the one-car garage at the back of the property. "Just gonna see to the Ford," he would say and lumber out to the white clapboard building. He would slide into the driver's seat, check a few dials on the dash, then pull out a purloined copy of *Photoplay* magazine from its hiding place under the driver's seat. He would ogle the racy cover of Jane Russell in a low-cut dress (what his wife would call a woman of ill repute). He'd read it with one eye on the two figures chatting beneath the apple tree, knowing that his wife, president of the Women's Christian Temperance Union and church organist, would not approve.

The importance of harmony. Getting just the right blend.

Mom turned her head and looked directly into my eyes. We made eye contact for the first time in a year. The corners of Mom's mouth pulled upward slightly in what was the closest thing to a smile I had seen in months. She rested her head gently on my shoulder. I was afraid to breathe too deeply, as if the intake of too much oxygen would alter this moment. I took tiny inhalations and tried to quiet my racing heart. If I could just be still, I knew I could make this moment last.

A telephone call pulled me from early morning sleep, "Your mother died in her sleep this morning. Just about a half-hour ago."

"Oh." I was coming awake to these words.

"You know," the voice seemed softer, kinder, now that she had given me the news, "we are required to give the family notification as soon after death as possible."

"Well, yes, of course." I heard myself say "of course," as if she had just told me the mail had arrived or the dishes needed to be washed.

"She died peacefully."

"Thank you for telling me that." I said, but what I meant was, *Good. It's over. I'm so glad she is out of that body.*

I hung up the phone, sat up and felt a strange sense of exhilaration for both of us. There were no tears this time. I had done all my grieving years ago when I took Mom to the neurologist and received the diagnosis. For three months after that I wept.

Mom was no longer tethered to her useless body. At the end she was curled in a fetal position in a bed with rails just like a crib. She was moving backward, backward in time to infancy, to a time when life was simple, pure. Harmonious.

Six burning bushes bordering the rear of the cemetery have turned Christmas-red now that the weather has cooled. They rise from red clay against green lawn. Foggy ridges of mountains fade in the distance. The burning bushes, their branches dense with tiny red berries, are a favorite of the birds. The wood thrush and wrens no longer favor the dogwood since it dropped its dense green leaves. The bare branches leave birds too vulnerable to hawks that fly above, scanning the ground for prey. The crape myrtle, though, is holding onto orange and copper colored leaves as if it were holding its breath this fall. The trunk and limbs are nearly smooth, the bark shedding, dropping in long, brown, pencil-like shavings curled at the base of the tree.

The bark on the tree next to the bench where I often sit still bears the long, deep scars gouged by a raccoon that died in its struggle to free itself after being trapped in the V of a branch. My Cherokee gardener told me that the raccoon is a sacrifice to the garden, a good omen. "The tree will have great power to do good for you and for the people you love," she said.

Geese fly in formation above me calling to each other with their distinctive honking. JB lifts his ears, looks up into the sky from his spot on the front lawn under the beech trees below the garden, throws his head back, and howls with displeasure. He is annoyed that they have disturbed his tranquility, but mostly I know he is upset because they are beyond his reach.

The garden below the cemetery is brown and dying. Spent plants release their progeny. Seed pods are scattered on the ground around the dying heads of plants. Day lily leaves turn yellow and fold over themselves with the effort of forcing food stored in the leaves down to the root to be absorbed for next year's growth.

Leaves scrunch beneath my feet, some still green, some mottled with red-brown stains, others dry and gray. It is quiet now. I wander the cemetery. No messages for me? Something whispered so quietly I do not hear? *Maybe it is time for the deep sleep winter will bring.* Sleep, my dear ones, sleep.

"Well. . . ," a long, silence hung in the air between the doctor's word and my oldest son, John, and me. We waited for him to speak.

Silence grew in the small examining room. "Well, I think," the doctor's, square jaw moved almost imperceptibly. The only clue to his bewilderment was his hesitant speech along with a slight jaw movement back and forth as his teeth tried to grind out a solution I knew he did not have. *Will he offer some new, bizarre treatment for my son's pain?* "Well," he began again, "we could try a morphine pump."

I wanted to scream: *Are you nuts? What the hell are you thinking? Do you have any idea what that will do to his chances of having any kind of life?* The words bounced around in my head, careening off the inside of my cranium like two boxers dancing in a ring trying to find the vulnerable spot on their opponent. My brain was crazy, busy being upset, while the rest of me sat quietly, mute, waiting for my son to speak.

Silence thickened in the tiny examining room. I wanted to move, pace, discharge this terrible nervous energy. *Is this room shrinking? Is it smaller than when we arrived minutes ago?*

Who the hell designed examining rooms, anyway? There was an implied intimacy in this close space I did not feel.

The long silence that followed seemed to immobilize us in our chairs. *Are we all playing that childhood game "Simon Says"? Whoever makes the first move loses. Be cool, John. Don't bite. Don't take the carrot he is dangling in front of your face.*

I looked at this decent-looking young internist and saw he had no idea what to do for my son. Not a clue. He had no idea how to treat his pain. Neither did all the other specialists and doctors we saw, so they passed John off to him.

John is a tough guy to treat even without Reflex Sympathetic Dystrophy (RSD), because medication for one of his neurological conditions can interfere with another. That, plus the way medicine is practiced in this country divides John's body into parts, a neurologist to treat one condition, a pain specialist for another, an internist, a psychologist, and a psychiatrist for other conditions. To complicate matters further, if the doctors aren't all in the same hospital system it's a challenge to get them to share information.

When John lived in Boston we were able to find good doctors all at Beth Israel Deaconess Medical Center. The neurologist there informally coordinated care. Then she left that hospital to practice elsewhere.

I remember my own experience: seeing a podiatrist, complaining of pain that seemed to be in my foot but sometimes seemed to travel up to my thigh. The podiatrist gently placed his hand on my calf. "My license stops here," he shrugged. "Maybe you ought to see an orthopedist." I stared at him dumbstruck and nearly laughed out loud at the absurdity of dividing my body into parts as if I were an automobile.

Today the doctor suggested treating John's RSD by masking

the pain. *Some treatment.* And, with *morphine.* In time, masking John's pain would silence my son, kill his spirit, steal his soul. *Madness!*

No one spoke and a more ominous silence stole into this tiny room, seeped from beneath the doorway like fog, crept around my ankles, moved up my calves to my knees, slipped like a belt too tightly cinched around my waist, pressed under my armpits, and engulfed my throat. I could not breathe.

John finally said, "I don't think so." He spoke just those four words. His eyes, filled with disappointment and lost hope, were downcast. *Despair. Despair that another doctor in this country, the United States, one of the wealthiest in the world, has no way to cure his pain.*

John had suffered a complex fracture of his left foot that was misdiagnosed, easy to miss on an x-ray because it was a *lis franc* fracture. A second x-ray showed the damage. Complex Regional Pain Syndrome or Reflex Sympathetic Dystrophy had developed several weeks after surgery.

No doctor we had seen seemed to be able to touch the pain. Nothing we had tried, not physical therapy, acupuncture, injections, or drugs, could put John's life back together.

My son turned and smiled at me slyly. He was doctor-wise, hospital-wise, by then. I wrapped my fingers around the sides of my thighs to remind myself: *Still your tongue. Still your hands. Let it come from him. This is his life. Even though he's only 24.*

The doctor picked up John's chart, thick with letters, lab tests, blood work from other referring doctors. He scribbled something quickly on the chart, "Maybe you'd like some time to think this over."

"No, I don't think so. Thanks."

"We have literature on the pump. I can have the nurse get you. . . ."

We were already out the door. We walked down the hallway toward the exit and the only sound I heard was the rhythmic tapping of John's cane as he leaned heavily on his bad leg. We escaped to the safety of my car.

A soft, classical symphony droned through the car radio. I could barely choke out the words, "Good decision." He reclined the passenger seat for the drive home, his body exhausted from the effort of rising, dressing, shaving, and traveling thirty minutes to this appointment. At twenty-four a morphine pump would mean his life was over. *At twenty-four.* We whizzed through a busy intersection, passing fast-food drive-ins, the signboards in primary colors, reds, oranges, yellows and blues, reminding us of youth, energy, verve, *fun.*

"You did well, JF." I slid into his old nickname for comfort, for a time that had been better, a time before Mom's illness had stolen her life. Mom had come for John's birth, staying three weeks. She had given John his first bath, cooked meals, did laundry, and let me nap whenever I could. "John Fredrick Lauritzen. Goodness, such a big name for a little guy," she said. "I'm going to call him JF. I like that. It's a better size for a newborn." She grinned at his rosebud face, swaddled him in a blanket and nested him in the crook of her arm.

I kept both hands on the steering wheel even though I wanted to pull over and swaddle JF in the little protection my love could offer him. I didn't speak. My throat swelled with tears. I swallowed them to keep my vision clear enough to drive home through the splash of fall color displayed by the foothills, an *Oktoberfest* of oranges, greens, reds and yellows.

WE WERE SITTING IN A CIRCLE, the three of us, me and my two sons. We were surrounded by large pieces of living room furniture: an overstuffed sofa, swivel chairs, a coffee table, end tables, lamp tables, big fluffy cushions. It was the same furniture we had in Chicago, the two big wing chairs I had found in a thrift shop with carved ball and claw feet (and cushions with real steel springs, not crummy foam), an oriental side bar with hidden drawers, and brass lamps with hummingbird finials, all so carefully chosen to make a life, a home, comfort. I believed bringing these pieces to North Carolina would replicate that same comfort. It did not. It brought familiarity and maybe a sort of sameness that I needed in a world that was becoming unfamiliar, alien.

I looked around at the three of us and it seemed as if we were in a circle of wagons in this desert of furniture. *Silly.* I don't know why this image was so powerful. *A wagon train in the middle of the living room.*

I had not entertained since John gave up his independent apartment, part-time job, and college. Now everything was upside down, shifted, *different.* His illness was running our lives, determining our schedule, consuming hours and days and weeks of time driving him to the best teaching hospitals in the South after the doctors in Boston sent him home. "He will do better around family," they said. *Right. Pass him off. What they meant was: that's all they had left to suggest. Well, he has always had family. Always. Will it be Enough?*

The voice of his brother, Jason, pulled me back to the circle, "Just consider it, John. It's Thanksgiving. You can let us know your decision after Christmas." Jason leaned forward in his chair and patted John's arm, mindful not to bump or touch his brother's leg or foot. Doing so would set off waves of pain.

I was silent. I folded my hands on my lap, hands that wanted to wrap themselves around these two sons, these precious gifts, these late-born sons of mine. *My heart.* I called them each that and they gave me that *Oh, Mom!* look, but they knew how fiercely I felt about them. My shallow breath made my stomach tight and achy. I felt the ache run through the long scar on my belly, the small price I paid for their births.

"Just think about it."

"But, *China,* Jason?"

I watched my two adult children negotiate. I made a tent of my fingers. Kept silent.

"You're not getting any better here. Look at you. Some days you need a wheelchair. A *wheelchair.*" Jason's voice rose and I saw him readjust his body in his chair, looking for an opening, trying to earn a moment, searching for another strategy. He was a tennis player in high school, I reminded myself as I watched him pull out old skills, and new ones, too, skills he had learned after losing his dad.

Jason was the one who cried inconsolably the night his father died, sobbing for hours. Then he went to sleep, woke up the next day and did not cry again. An all-consuming depression replaced his tears and filled the hole in his life. He sank deeper into his unexpressed grief, did less and less and when he finally could not get out of bed to go to school, I suggested that he should see a therapist.

"Don't need it." He stormed out of the kitchen and back to his bedroom.

I dragged him to the car and strapped him into his seat belt. "You have to go four times. After that, we'll talk about how you are doing."

He refused to speak to me and stared straight ahead on

the drive to the therapist's office. I knew I was doing the right thing. I wasn't *Enough*. After four sessions, Jason wrote a letter to his father and sealed it in an envelope. He took the envelope to Sweet Woods Garden and put it on Henry's gravestone, holding it in place with a rock. It stayed there for a year, the envelope becoming wrinkled and rippled with weathering. After that, he seemed better and could go to school and study and his appetite returned.

Jason had learned about doing hard things. About what grit is. About going on when it doesn't seem possible. At twenty, I knew he had the grit to help John through this.

Jason lowered his voice to make his request seem reasonable. What we were both suggesting was that John leave everything he knew, all that gave him what little comfort it could, and fly half-way around the world for treatment.

"All right. I'll think about it," John looked at Jason, then stared at his offending left foot. He frowned. I wondered if he saw it as I did, an uninvited guest in our wagon train circle.

The decision was left all of the Christmas holiday like the unwanted present beneath the Christmas tree. The anxiety like opening a gift from the neighbor we barely know who doesn't know what we like.

A PHONE CALL CAME from the international program in China in response to our request, "The doctors said they cannot promise anything, but they will do their best. They will take him." My tears spilled onto the phone's handset as I heard the voice of an American nurse whose healing experience in China was so successful that she was now taking Americans there for treatment. She told me that they treat each patient's whole body, using integrative medicine, six hours a day, six days a week for a minimum of ninety days. It felt right. I trusted this. For the first time in eighteen months, my son was accepted, taken in. *No longer a throw away.*

A deep sigh resonated through my body as I sensed the Chinese have the only ingredient that matters: willingness. I was willing, too. I was willing to send John to China. I was willing to encourage John to step off the edge of the world. *Anything. Save him.* I didn't know these people, but I would send my heart to China, to a place I had never been, to people I had never met. The voice at the other end of the telephone spoke the language of compassion, a language I could understand, a language John and I both needed to hear.

"Finally." Jason relaxed his chin that had been pulled tight and his face softened. His slender body loosened as if it had been held in one of those unnatural postures for team tennis shots. "Sanity. Let's go for it."

The next weeks were busy with passports, visa letters, packing, longing. It was surreal. *I am sending my son away from me when he needs me so much. I am not Enough. Yes, that's right. I am sending my son away because he needs so much.*

Tuesday. A hoarfrost, silver and gray, outlines the black wrought-iron gate at the cemetery entrance. I touch it with the tip of my gloved fingers (as curious at sixty-seven as I was at seven), and the frost collapses between my fingers, then dissolves into a pile of ice crystals at my feet. Even the miniature azalea leaves at the

foot of the bench are fuzzy, their tips frost-coated. A trail of boot marks follows me, imprints in the sheen of gray frost filming the yellowed grass.

Five brass markers set on speckled gray and white marble are unmarked by frost. It is as if they are saying this ground is sacred, special, and will remain untouched by the seasons.

A few energetic sparrows chirp in the distance. In the field below the cemetery the McCrearys' cows moo mournfully, unhappily foraging along the icy bank of the French Broad River ankle-deep in snow. I feel it, too. The chill penetrates my woolen pants and the tips of my fingers grow cold within my gloves.

From the corner of my eye I see JB pacing back and forth in the front yard waiting for me. He is watchful, ever hopeful that the squirrel above his head will leave his nest, try to scale the branches of the beech tree, make a misstep, and become his prey.

I lean forward to unhook the Christmas wreath I had hung on the cemetery gate, a wreath of pine cones scattered among Fraser fir attached to a grapevine circle. The red bow is furry with frost. I detach it. "Until next Christmas," I say, nodding toward the five graves. I turn around, face the house, and walk toward it with the wreath swaying from its hook. The wreath swings back and forth in my hand, its motion in cadence with my boot steps.

I'm reminded of the motion of the swinging incense burners, the thuribles I had seen my Catholic cousins, eleven-year-old altar boys, carry. I can see those scruffy cousins dressed in pristine surplices (their unruly cowlicks smoothed) with their short robes swinging side to side as they walk behind the priest.

The smell of incense mingles with the scent of pine and my cold breath. My wreath swinging, the altar boys' thuribles swinging, each of us honoring a sacred moment.

WEDNESDAY. THE WORLD IS SILENT, still. Nothing moves. Snow fell all night long, stilling the world, blanketing everything. It is as if the world is covered in a dense cotton blanket muffling pain, loss, laughter, sorrow. The sky is pale gray, cloudless. The contrast of gray and white only makes the snow seem brighter, bright enough to make me squint.

I pass the scotch broom at the edge of the small flower bed at the top of the hill and notice how this small bush struggles to remain upright in a heavy snowfall, unprecedented in the South. Her boughs lie in the snow, defeated both by weather and my arrogance for planting such a vulnerable plant at the highest, windiest, most open spot on my property. Just for my pleasure. My vanity. Just because I want to view thousands of tiny, yellow blossoms from the vantage point of my front door in springtime. I probably will lose it this spring for not having the good sense to plant this tender shrub in a more protected spot. I am not reasonable when it comes to gardening.

The big oaks beyond the cemetery have lost their leaves and the branches are coated with an icing of snow. The crape myrtle in Sweet Woods Garden is frosted with snow that conceals the desperate racoon's claw marks. Snow has temporarily erased her history. The cemetery is a whitewash, leaving just the slightest indentation above each grave marker to indicate the place where the graves lie. "We're still here! Don't forget," the markers seem to say.

I turn to go back to the house, trudging through knee-deep snow. I laugh when I look back and see the crazy zigzag path that my unsteady southern legs have made. My sturdy northern legs have relaxed in warm weather and grown slack and lazy in this climate. The only sound I hear as I return to the warmth of the house is the crunch-crunch of my boots as they break through the snow's icy crust.

It is unusually peaceful and quiet today. I feel silence soothe me and realize how all my life I have loved the quiet. Actually, it's my preference. This day, this absolute stillness is like a prayer, a meditation and I suck in great gulps of it. Then I realize. Of course! That's it! I get it. The first eighteen months of my life. Of course.

Those early years of my parents' marriage set the tone, when they had lived in a rental apartment in Indianapolis, Indiana, near the end of World War II, just after I was born. Due to the war effort, Dad had been relocated by his company to work in a manufacturing plant there. Mom and Dad had found the furnished, second-story apartment in an elderly woman's house at a time when finding housing was nearly impossible. Mom was left alone on the second floor of a house in a neighborhood where she knew no one. She dusted expensive mahogany antiques she didn't own, remembering the words the landlady spoke as they paid their first month's rent: "I prefer not to rent to a couple with children, but as long as you keep her quiet and away from the furniture you can rent it."

Dad was rarely there except to come home, eat, sleep, and return to another fifteen-hour workday, six days a week. Mom's attitude was: "We'll make do."

So we lived in a sort of muffled silence. I remember her rolling her long hair into a coil on top of her head, tying a broad-brimmed bonnet on mine, bundling me in blankets and pushing me through the park on the silent, rubber wheels of a pale green pram. I peeked out from a tiny space left for my eyes and nose beneath the blankets and saw tree tops and my mother's sorrowful brown eyes.

Dad was transferred to Chicago when I was two years old. Every Sunday we drove the twenty-five minutes from the relative quiet of our home to the clamor and hubbub at Grandma's. It was a noisy house full of Italians who all spoke at once, hands gesturing, their bodies in constant motion as if trying to keep time with some secret rhythm I did not understand.

This shift in my life startled and stunned me. I became shy and hesitant, craved quiet and clung to my mother. Looking back at old black and white Kodak photos, I see images of myself, a small blond child, peeking from behind my mother's skirts. *Cautious. Silent.*

The images stir memories of my childhood home, the one my parents bought in the southern suburbs of Chicago in 1945 and owned for twenty-five years. The living room had a freestanding AM/FM Magnavox radio console that also played thirty-three and a third and seventy-eight rpm records. In the late afternoon Mom played Mantovani's recordings of "Three Coins in the Fountain," "Melodia De Amor," and waltzes. The purpose of the music was to put Mom in the mood for cooking and put Dad right when he returned from a long workday in downtown Chicago. Music soothed, filled the silence.

At the dining room table, music filtered in as family members spoke one at a time, in a different rhythm from Grandma's house. At our house we each reported on our day: "I have a spelling test tomorrow" or "The train ride home was long. Something about another train breaking down near Monroe Street" or "I'm not sure about the pot roast, the regular butcher was sick and his helper cut it." Mantovani's "Moon River" droned on, filling the quiet between reports.

The dining room opened onto the back yard and had double casement windows that cranked out. The windows were open even though the weather was cool for October. Ivy covered the back of our red-brick house. The casement windows were the only visible openings in the dense, green mass. Dad knew the ivy would eventually pull the mortar away from the house, but Mom loved the look: "We are all so tucked in and cozy, don't you think?"

Then. *Thunk. Thunk.* We all heard the thuds.

"Another one. Can we go and see?" I asked. A bird had flown into the glass looking for an opening in the ivy and lay dead or stunned on the ground below.

"After dinner. Finish your meal first," Mom instructed. My brother's legs swung back and forth in anticipation. I knew he was thinking about that bird, wondering if it were dead. *Will we have to find a box, get a shovel, and bury it?* Mom cleared the table and nodded to us. "You can do the dishes after you've checked on the bird, okay?" Paul and I raced out the back door.

The door banged, the music stopped playing, and the only sound in the house was the click of the arm on the record player as it automatically returned to its off position.

THAT WAS IT. The decision was made. We would move from Chicago's big urban noise and jagged skyscrapers lining the lakefront to a tiny town of single-story buildings nestled in the soft curves of the Blue Ridge Mountains. *Our Mayberry.* We craved quiet country life, a place for Henry to be away from the frigid Chicago winters that depleted his immune system and sent him to the hospital all too often with infections. A place with good schools for the boys. A place that offered quality life.

My body unwound and loosened in the simple rhythm of small-town life. My father called, "How is the new house? Do you like your neighbors? Good." He would be coming to visit next week. He stayed three days, loved it, too, and announced the day he returned to his apartment in a retirement community in Arkansas, "I'm moving to North Carolina, to be with you and the boys. The family should be together." *Together? We haven't lived in the same state in twenty-seven years.*

Never mind that he would be leaving his wife of sixty-five years, *my mother*, in Arkansas in a skilled nursing facility. Never mind that Mom was trapped inside her shriveled body, tangled in the crossed wires of altered brain chemistry. He never visited her. He couldn't bear the weight of her illness, its pressure like a hand squeezing his chest each time he approached the doors of the skilled nursing wing.

He told me, "My sisters visit her twice a week," as they had since she went in. "They'll keep me posted." Never mind that his current companion, a woman who accompanied Dad on several cruises, had just been diagnosed with breast cancer and needed him, too.

Dad's move to North Carolina was his way of escaping having to face the last years of Mom's decline and he landed squarely on his feet with every one of his character defects, avarice, lust and covetousness, operating full tilt. Maribel's small-town, conservative upbringing, her Victorian parents, his childhood and adolescence in the Catholic Church all fell by the wayside as he spent his last years living an unrestrained life.

It had always been difficult to hear about his behavior second-hand through my aunts when he lived near them, but it would be worse now that I would be living it in first person. Nothing could rein him in. Not the memory of his wife,

Maribel, the regard of the community, or the reputation of his son and daughter living in the same town (where I was an officer in the church he would attend).

Dad had spent his early years pleasing others, doing the right thing. No longer. That was over. After all, he had a track record for being an upstanding guy. He was the one who, after arguing for days with his siblings, had committed his older sister, my aunt Mini, to a mental hospital when her depression became suicidal. He was the one who had pushed the decision to place his mother in a nursing home, "What, John! Ma? No! Never!" In time, though, he was patted on the back and told it was the best decision the family ever made.

He had helped many nephews network and find jobs through his professional connections, remembering the time during the Depression when he was the sole family member working. Everyone respected Uncle Johnny. He was the "Godfather."

But now it was as if he were done, done making decisions, and choosing instead to follow his every proclivity.

Even though Mom lingered seven more years in the nursing home, he declared her somehow "not there" and with it, ended that part of his life. *The hell with propriety and being a stand-up guy.* At least he hung onto the vestiges of his old self, dressing well, speaking well, showing up for Sunday dinner, but the obstinate little boy who had sat at his mother's table in Caspian, Michigan, and had refused to remove his cap at dinner was out, running free, waving his hat in his hand.

I received the call late one afternoon. "Pick out an apartment at the retirement center just down the street from your place," he ordered. "I'll be there in three weeks. And, by the way, find me a one bedroom that faces a view of the French

Broad River. I want to be on the water." *Better for late night drownings.* I felt the ease of country living evaporating from every pore of my body.

He arrived just a day before the moving van, walked into a one-bedroom apartment with a view of the French Broad and a life where he was one of the few single men in the complex. He described the place, "Just like the Wild West," where the ratio of men to women was much like the ratio of cowboys to Indians and he threw his hat in the ring. Competition for a man who was upright, lucid, and ambulatory was fierce, and Dad met most of the qualifications.

The casserole brigade appeared on Day One. Sweet, little, blue-haired ladies, many of whom were members of the church where I was an officer, lined up at the door with all manner of goodies. Somehow through their elaborate communication system they already knew his favorites. They welcomed him with oatmeal raisin cookies on the soft side, soups, tiny, carefully decorated cupcakes, and casseroles (layers of unknown canned substances covered with a toppings of crushed potato chips) still warm from the oven.

He accepted it all with élan, his full head of silver hair shining and wearing his best cruise wear, polyester slacks, white wingtips, a casual knit shirt, and a bolo (selected from his collection of thirty bolos) that dangled just below his collar.

Dinner was hours away. The casserole ladies lined the hallway outside his door, a study in unashamed competition. These women could no longer compete for Miss America or even Mrs. America, but they were *survivors*. They had lived through World War I, World War II, the Korean War, Vietnam, their husbands and their children.

Dad turned down not a single one, "Oh, my favorite! Tuna

noodle. Just like Stouffer's frozen brand. Maybe I won't have to struggle to get to the grocery store." His own white teeth flashed his best smile. He set the casseroles on the sideboard just inside his apartment door. "You know my wife, Maribel, was a great cook," he sighed, paused meaningfully for emphasis and pressed the folded handkerchief he pulled from his pants pocket to his cheek. Several of the women in line asked to borrow his handkerchief to wipe their own eyes, so taken were they by his performance.

DAD HAD COME A LONG WAY from the small mining town in Caspian, Michigan, where he grew up, the son of an Italian immigrant. His father was a company man who worked all day feeding the furnaces of the Verona Mining Company, returning home at dusk to his company-owned house, without plumbing, to my grandmother and ten kids. Six of the ten were girls.

My father was born in the middle of the six girls. He was reared by his Italian sisters who spoiled all the men in the family, cooking, cleaning, ironing their shirts, and scrubbing their backs in the big tub that sat on the back porch, while theirs ached.

Dad developed two opinions of the world as a result of his early experiences, before the family's move to Chicago when he was twelve. One was entitlement. He had a birthright to be cared for by women. The other was a survival skill he developed in growing up around so many sisters. He managed any conflict with a woman by offering a healthy dose of silence. If he couldn't win, he'd stonewall.

Dad glanced over his shoulder at the women in line at the front door. It was three o'clock, time to cull one of the women for dinner. A short, petite woman approached. A black cloth embroidered with deep red roses covered her basket of homemade sweet rolls. She lifted the cloth as he held the basket in his hand.

"Don't know if you go for sweet things, John."

"Oh, yes, definitely," another flash of his pearly whites. She met many of his requirements for a companion – no assisted devices for ambulating, dresses well, and wears makeup beautifully applied to her soft skin. But, did she own a car?

"Oh, good. I hope you won't be disappointed in my small offering."

Dad's eyes rose from the basket to her breasts. "Not in the least."

"My name is Linda. I live just around the corner." She pointed over her shoulder down the hallway. "Close by."

"Been here long?"

"No. Just moved in myself from South Carolina. I had to give up the lake house, three cars, the maid. It was just too much."

Dad's brown eyes grew round and opened wider.

"What a shame. Too bad. But *c'est la vie*, eh, Linda?"

"Yes, but I did have the wall taken out between two apartments to get all my antiques in the new place. It seems to be working out. I kept one car."

"You drive?"

Each Sunday I collected all of them for Sunday dinner: Dad with his double knee replacement, his cane and two beeping hearing aids and my two ancient aunts, his older sisters. They had ridden from Arkansas to North Carolina wedged between a third aunt, Eda, in the back seat of my cousin's car to attend a family reunion. They announced at the end of the reunion that they weren't going home. "That's it. We're staying. My bladder can't take the trip back," declared the oldest, pounding the dining room table for emphasis. My aunts each had walkers, one had hearing aids in both ears; her sister, a single aid. The oldest was nearly blind. They were all in their nineties.

My brother Paul moved here as well and joined us for Sunday dinner. Living at the highest elevation in the county, in Christmas tree country a half-hour away, he would drive down the winding, two-lane road in his truck. My brother, younger by four years, had re-located to North Carolina with his wife of twenty-five years. She decided she liked the big city and their retirement savings better than the mountains and returned to Houston, leaving my brother with peace of mind, clear well water to drink, and not much cash.

I became re-acquainted with my brother. Three mornings a week, when we were kids, he would split the eggs we ate for breakfast. He liked the white. I ate the yolks. My brother, Paul, as a child, disassembled vacuum cleaners, clocks and other household appliances and reassembled them perfectly without needing an instruction manual, but he could not sit still in school and barely passed his classes. Paul became a first-rate mechanic, raced formula cars for Ford, and made three times what I ever earned. He was a volunteer fire chief in Spring, Texas, for twenty years and saw more pain, loss and death as a fireman and paramedic than Dad could ever imagine. The son who did not go to college did not fit Dad's concept of what the only son of a first generation immigrant should be. Paul, too, I believe, inherited the *Not Enough* legacy.

Despite the pressure, rejection, and disappointment, he has remained easy-going, bright and able to fix anything. I always envy him because he can see the results of his labor materialize before his eyes, a sort of evidence of worth. My abilities have no such gauge. People warm to him easily, finding Paul approachable in flannel shirts, jeans and work shoes. What he can't say in words, he expresses in repairing a squeaky screen door, checking the tire pressure on my car, getting the toilet to stop running, sharpening the blades on my riding mower.

My two sons were still living at home and at Sunday dinner watched as old rivalries surfaced, observing adults behave no differently from the way they had as toddlers.

After an interminable period of time manipulating walkers and canes into the dining room, guiding each older member of the family into comfortable chairs, I took my seat at the head of the table, certainly *not* because I felt I was running the show here, but because it was closest to the kitchen and the stove. As I slid into my padded chair, I hoped that none of them heard the audible sigh of relief whoosh from my lips.

"I have to go to the bathroom," one of my aunts bleated just as I set the last steaming bowl of soup at her place.

"I like my soup hot," my father ignored his sister's departure from the table and picked up his spoon. I hoped that the

soup's heady aroma would mute the sharp edges of tension between my father and his older sisters.

"Dad. We haven't said grace yet," I said to buy time until
the table was complete again.

"I went to church this morning," the old Italian croaked.
My sons looked at each other and grinned, amused that an
adult was at the center of my censure.

"Honestly, John," his other sister chirped, "This is the one
day of the week the family gets together. You could at least. . . ,"
she stopped right there, put her hands on her lap, pursed her
lips and glared at my father. In one deft motion he had raised
both hands to his ears, flipped off his hearing aids, reached for
the bowl of freshly grated Asiago cheese at his elbow and liber-
ally sprinkled his soup. Dad lifted the golden broth to his lips.
My brother and I eyed each other knowingly: *this meal was like
so many meals before.* Then, too, there was that ring of truth
from another lunch I had shared with Dad.

I RACED UP THE CEMENT STEPS at the Ivanhoe Street Station
and managed just to land my feet in the last car of the Illinois
Central as the train pulled away from the station. I fell side-
ways into the yellow, caned back seat. My bottom hit the cush-
ion with a thump. I laughed out loud, both from the bump
and in anticipation of the day ahead.

Next to me on the seat was a copy of the *Chicago Tribune*
folded back to expose the crossword puzzle, nearly completed.
I unfolded the paper, scanned the horoscope column for my
sign, Leo. It read: "You long for independence and autono-
my. Today has a fresh air feeling. Talk about your values and

beliefs." I followed my horoscope, reading it first in jest as something to laugh about on the bus ride to high school, but now with a certain curiosity about the ring of truth the readings held. This day, the breath of fresh air was this trip downtown to have lunch with Dad.

"Where to today?" the conductor, in a navy blue uniform and cap, greeted me. As the train shifted, he easily dispensed nickels, dimes, quarters and pennies from the metal changer on his belt with the nimble fingers of his right hand. A fistful of single dollar bills swayed in the other. He stood with his feet apart, leaning on the backs of his black shoes to keep his balance as the train moved forward. The conductor's voice pulled me from images of a quiet lunch with Dad across a table for two.

"Oh! Sorry! Randolph. Round trip, please."

I handed the conductor the bills as he punched paper tickets and clipped them to the seat back in front of me.

"Your change, Miss. Looks like you're going to be late for work today. Or are you just keeping banker's hours?" I was surprised, then smiled, flattered that the conductor viewed me as an older, working woman.

"Just a day in the Loop." Today was a high school holiday and I was doing research for my senior project at the main library in downtown Chicago.

As the conductor moved on, I slid toward the window and opened it. Although the weather outside was autumn cool and crisp, the air inside the car was stale and dusty. I leaned my elbow against the window and looked down from the elevated tracks at the rooftops flying past.

I would graduate in May and be the first in my family to attend a four-year college. *All the sacrifices my parents' made to pay for my private college education!* Mom went back to work several years ago. Family vacations were limited to simple fishing trips in Wisconsin. *What if I flunked out? Hated it?* I knew I would miss long, lazy conversations late at night with Mom. Dad talked about how he was counting on me to make them proud. *What about living away from home?* Trips away had been limited to Grandma's and to camp. Both made me homesick and apprehensive. The one appealing element of being away at school was not having every boy I dated scrutinized by Dad.

"115th Street—Kensington!" The conductor called out the stop as the train moved into the station. I pulled my book bag close and retrieved my project outline.

"Washington!" The next stop was mine. I made some hasty notes in the margin of the outline and slid my work into the bag.

The trip to Randolph Street aroused fond memories of childhood excursions to Chicago with favorite aunts. Most memorable was our annual trip at Christmastime to the Walnut Room at Marshall Field's for lunch followed by a magical tour of the animated displays in store windows. Once again I was looking forward to being the focus of a beloved adult's undivided attention.

It was the first time I had met Dad in the city alone. Dad's leisure time was a precious commodity and he spent much of it with all of us. His work took him out of town often and when he was in town he worked late at the office several nights a week. My fingers drummed the armrest and my feet tapped on the train floor as the train came to a halt.

"Randolph! End of the line."

My research at the library went quickly. I stepped into the ladies' room before leaving the building to check my hair in the mirror and smooth away any wrinkles in my outfit that Mom had just finished sewing. The turquoise tweed skirt and coordinated turquoise blouse complimented my skin. I had just finished pulling a brush through my hair and was examining my appearance in the mirror when I remembered the article I read in "Seventeen" about dressing for success. I reached into my purse, pulled out a half-dozen bobby pins and a rubber band. Even though Mom said this article was for working women, just for today I would wear my hair in this new way.

Dad suggested we meet at Don Roth's Blackhawk Restaurant a block from the library. I checked my watch and sped out the door. Bright sunlight and the clamor of noisy downtown traffic greeted me. Cabs zipped up to the curb from nowhere to pick up rides, buses groaned past, and a sea of people bustled along the sidewalks. Professional women, whom I imagined worked in banks or attorneys' offices, passed me in tailored suits and matching handbags. They seemed focused and self-possessed. I wondered if going away to school would magically produce that air of confidence in me.

I entered the restaurant. It took a moment for my eyes to adjust to the darkened room. Hurricane lamps lit the burgundy cloth-covered tables while small wall sconces provided the only other illumination. Piano music played softly in the background as I watched the head waiter seat men and women at tables. Waiters stood at several tables mixing the restaurant's famous "Spinning Bowl" salad dressing. The aroma of anchovies, olive oil, fresh, ground pepper and lemon juice sharpened my appetite.

This was the first time I had walked into a fancy restaurant alone. I stood feeling awkward, shy and uncomfortable, that child hiding behind my mother's skirts still dogging me at times like this. The head waiter moved toward me. I forced myself to smile, although I wanted to tug at the hem of my skirt.

"Miss? Do you have a reservation?"

I stepped back and then felt a steady hand on my shoulder. "Dad!"

In his breezy, confident fashion he leaned down and gave me a kiss on the cheek.

The waiter smiled, "Mr. Carraro! Nice to see you again. Your regular table?"

Dad nodded, grasped my elbow and led me to our table. "This is fine. Thank you, Earl."

Dad pulled out a chair, "Here's a special seat for a special young lady today. New hairdo?" His hand squeezed my shoulder as sat down. I felt the little girl hiding behind her mother's skirts fade.

"Did you get your research done or do you have to return after lunch for a second round?" He seated himself, unbuttoned his suit jacket and slid a cloth napkin across his legs.

The waiter handed us menus. "We're gong to need a moment, thanks."

Dad turned to me. "I see Mom finally finished sewing that outfit, honey. She sure burned the midnight oil for that one, eh? Is this the first time you've worn it or have you already knocked the socks off some guy at school with that outfit?"

"Oh, Dad!" I felt myself blush and smoothed my hand over my skirt. "No one says 'knock-your-socks-off' anymore! Dave, this new guy I am interested in, seemed to notice it at school earlier this week. Oh, I don't know." I reddened again.

"Now that sounds promising. Is this the one you wanted to ask you to the Prom?"

"No! *Dave* is the one I'm interested in."

"Oh, yes. I remember him. Funny guy. Wasn't he at the splash party we had at your birthday last year?"

"No. He wasn't there." *I wish he would quit getting the names of the boys mixed up and just, well, I don't know, admire my choices, tell me I have good judgment, and be the listener Mom is.* Conversations with Dad seemed awkward and made me feel unsettled.

In spite of my awkwardness I could hardly contain my delight at not having to share this table with my brother, who always disrupted conversation with goofy facial gestures or embarrassing sounds, or Mom, whose priority was being reassured that everyone was pleased with what they were eating.

Dad leaned forward, placed his elbows on the arms of his captain's chair, folded his fingers together and faced me directly, telling me he was giving me his full attention. It was the same gesture he offered his own mother on Sundays. A place in the center of me warmed and settled. I relaxed in my chair and looked over the menu.

As Dad eyed the menu, two men in business suits walked past. One was tall and slender, the other shorter with a broad chest. Dad looked up, then rose to meet them.

"John! Good to see you!" The tall man spoke first, extending his hand.

They shook hands, then turning, Dad said, "Jeff, Tim, this is my daughter, Karen. Honey, I'd like you to meet Mr. Bosley, our chief engineer and his assistant, Mr. McDonald."

My heart sank. *There goes my special time.*

"Oh, I see our table is ready. Nice to have met you, Karen." The shorter man's eyes traveled the length of my blouse, lingering at my breasts, making me feel as uncomfortable as I felt when boys leered at me in study hall. Both men moved to their table.

"Now, let's see where we were, honey." As Dad sat down, his napkin slid to the floor and he bent to retrieve it.

I looked at the men who had stopped nearby to let the waiter pass. They were close enough that I heard Mr. Bosley say to Mr. McDonald, "His daughter? Sure! Right!" They both laughed and moved away.

I wondered if I had heard correctly. *Why would Mr. Bosley say that? Who did he think I was?* My stomach clenched. I frowned.

A vision of my parents made me question why Mom spent so much time late at night in the sewing room at the top of the stairs, why my parents didn't hold hands when they took an evening stroll like the other neighbors did. I lifted my eyes to Dad, *my dad*, who worked nights, who traveled. Why had Mr. Bosley's comments stirred these images?

I thought about the horoscope reading: "Talk about your values and beliefs." *What was going on here?* I set my glass of water down, feeling just slightly off balance. The softly padded chair suddenly felt hard, unforgiving, the noise in the room, too loud, the soft, romantic lighting, dark and gloomy.

Dad retrieved his napkin and his hand reached across the table, startling me from my thought. "I think I'll have a Rob Roy. What about you, honey? A Coke?"

"Father, sure, I'll have a Coke with my lunch."

"'Father'? What ever happened to dear old 'Dad'?"

"I've decided that from now on I'm calling you 'Father'. And you can call me 'Daughter'." The smells coming from the kitchen that, a few moments ago, tempted me, now turned my stomach.

HIS FINGERS SKIMMED THE PAGES he had written more than forty-five years ago, *"We have, in the following pages, attempted*

to picture . . . ," and, *"Even to the layman it must be apparent that.
. . ."* He flipped the book closed and patted the black binder
lettered in gold marked "Construction and Engineering Report
for Period November 1, 1945 to October 31, 1951." The binder
was just one of many he kept in his desk files along with glossy
black and white photos of himself with his hair clipped in a crew
cut and wearing a black suit, narrow knit black tie and white
shirt, standing alongside the big boys, the company executives,
where he worked for forty-one years. All his accolades had been
neatly cataloged, re-lived anytime he needed a boost. Re-reading
those words was as comforting to him as pulling on the heavy
wool socks he wore nearly every day, year round. (He had lousy
circulation, especially in his feet.)

Reviewing the bulk of his life and feeling the weight of it
in his hands, his measured success, he could almost feel those
handshakes and pats on the back again and hear the secretaries
greet him, "Why, good morning, Mr. Carraro." He had saved it
all. Every word, photograph, letters of congratulations, and the
pins he wore on the lapel of his black suit for ten years of service,
for twenty-five, then thirty, then forty.

He sighed and shifted in his favorite recliner. He wondered
if things would have been different if he had treated his wife
of sixty-five years with that same care. Always that sharp stab
of regret whenever Maribel's name rose above the thick wool
blanket of denial he spread across his world.

*Today her name seemed to float between the notes of the soft piano
music playing on the stereo in the background, regret slipping between the cadences of his carefully planned life. His breath caught*

*in his chest. He was feeling new riffs in the music that he knew
so well and counted on to keep him floating above his uncluttered
view of the past.*

HE LOOKED AROUND HIS CHAIR, viewing all the stuff of his
current life, the things he had chosen for his apartment that
gave him comfort. His stereo played soothing classical piano
on the nights he couldn't sleep, blotting out daytime memories
of transgressions. Scatter rugs placed strategically on the hard-
wood floor cushioned his steps as he crossed from living room
to bedroom. His bedroom closet was lined with twenty pairs of
shoes, a reminder of his affluence. *No hand-me-down, worn-out
leather boots from his older brother. No, sir!*

On the walls were his wife's paintings. *Her* worldly suc-
cesses. He drew satisfaction from her landscapes, many from
photographs he took on their trips to Europe, travels across the
United States, and their world cruise. *How well his life turned
out.* Often, when faced with the blank, empty hole Maribel had
left, he would fill that dark space by looking at her paintings,
at an arch over a building in Italy, a sunset in Spain, or rows of
corn fields in Illinois. Or, he would pull a book of poems down
from the bookshelf next to his recliner, let it fall open to Keats,
Byron or Shelley, slip beneath the cocoon of words, and not
think about the seven years his wife had been locked up, a dark
stranger inhabiting her spirit.

He had been everywhere, done it all. He rose as the son
of an Italian immigrant to be somebody. He had begun as a
draftsman, rose through the ranks, and became a project engineer, designing the first fully air-conditioned, truck assembly

plant in the United States. But none of that mattered, did it? Except, to help pass the time in evening conversation around the tables in the retirement center's dining room.

What he really needed and what he missed most was the sociability of his marriage. He needed, almost compulsively, to replicate that. So he was taking his pick of the many single women where he lived. He already had had half a dozen "companions," as he called them. Heart disease, diabetes, dementia had taken their toll on his pool of those available.

He had gone from his mother's house into his marriage. He had no idea how to live alone. He never was alone except for those horrible months early in their marriage when Maribel left him, went back home to her family in southern Illinois, stubbornly stayed, and made him live solo. She refused any communication but his hand written letters. He made promises that he had to keep so she would return. He would not think about that. It was the one time in their marriage that she had been better at stonewalling than he.

He rose and changed the music on the CD player to one of his favorite country singers. He loved Patsy Cline and Eddie Arnold. This time, Eddie Arnold was singing "Release me and let me love again." A sob escaped from his lips before he caught it. He sucked it back and wiped his lips with the back of his hand.

ON THE WALL ABOVE HIS CHAIR, my father had placed family photographs, not out of sentimentality, well, maybe yes, partially, but mostly because he liked to remind himself that there was always *la famiglia*, obligated to love him no matter what.

From early on, the family ritual of the meal had become as much a part of his life as his need to have a master chef prepare it. His Italian mother had rolled her own pasta dough and made sauces from scratch. During his working years, he had eaten his lunch either in the company's executive dining room or as his client's guest at a fine restaurant in downtown Chicago. His wife, Maribel, had learned to be a gourmet cook. After retiring at sixty, his twice-yearly cruises (a lifetime total of twenty-two) had acquainted him with the best ship kitchens.

Each new woman friend was required to turn out a good meal, possess a valid driver's license and an operational car so they could leave the retirement center several times a week and eat at a restaurant in town. It didn't hurt if the companion dressed well. He liked walking into a place with a good-looking woman on his arm with whom he could have a pleasant conversation across the table.

This month he was between companions, sans car, sans cook. He had returned from his latest cruise only to have his current companion complain of chest pain as soon as the plane landed. A trip to the doctor revealed that both her carotid arteries were blocked. The companion had a known history of diabetes which she had not bothered to mention before the trip, "Didn't want him to worry." They had both indulged in daily afternoon chocolate sundaes on the Soda Shoppe deck in addition to their regularly scheduled five squares a day on their cruise. "After all, we were off the coast of Florence on vacation," she explained to me, her eyes glazed. I had difficulty knowing if the look she had was the result of diabetes or my father. She was hustled from her independent apartment to the assisted living facility next door and to a salt-free, low-fat diet.

Dad was faced with preparing his own breakfast and lunch in his apartment. The main dining room would continue to provide his dinner, although he didn't like the current chef, "Too bland. The food's too bland. And what? No soup course?"

His love of food extended to mail ordering kitchen appliances, promoting the illusion he would someday use them to prepare a gourmet meal. Purchasing the food preparation utensils seemed to be his way of reliving memories of a good meal. Still in their shipping containers stacked around the apartment were a pasta machine, tomato press, double boiler, complete set of strangely-shaped, microwave cookware, a pizza pan, doughnut maker and set of whisks in graduated sizes.

He complained to any and all at my Sunday dinners about the quality and selection of food at the retirement center. It really wasn't that the food was poorly prepared or tasted badly. It was simply institutional cooking. "Too dry. No sauce." He said he longed for roast chicken with crisp, oven-browned skin, swimming in golden gravy, "Not that lousy, naked chicken breast, *skinless, for God's sake*, served on a piece of lettuce. *What's the chef thinking?*"

Tonight he would have what he wanted. He called a neighbor who lived several doors down from his apartment and asked her to pick up a whole chicken when she went to the grocery store that afternoon. Tonight he would cook to please himself. Of course it wouldn't be the five courses he was used to, but it would be good food, *buono, gustoso*. He wished the residents' community garden were still in season so he could collect zucchini blossoms to fry as an appetizer.

He smiled as he remembered picking blossoms from the garden he planted across the street from the home in which he and Maribel had lived for twenty-five years. He put the closed blossoms into a brown paper sack, twisted the top, and placed them in the vegetable bin at the bottom of the Frigidaire. Maribel would find them at dinnertime.

My mother grew up in a southern Illinois' farm town where she had served meatloaf, mashed potatoes and peas, all in one course, all on one plate. My father grew up in a rambling apartment on the south side of Chicago with six sisters and a mother who had cooked old-country Italian: simmering sauce (a permanent fixture on the stove's back burner), homemade *Chianti*, freshly baked *Cornetti* rolls. Maribel learned after they were married that Italians served meals of at least three courses. Fried zucchini flowers were a prized delicacy and served as a *primo* course.

"Oh. Antipasto. Another course." She dragged the brown bag from the crisper only to find, once opened, her kitchen full of very angry, very cold bees that had been trapped inside the closed flowers. They buzzed angrily over her head. *Her* introduction to bees as a child involved watching them pollinate hollyhocks that grew along the back fence of her childhood home. She sighed as she dipped the flowers in batter.

DAD CALLED ME TO GET the chicken roasting recipe he remembered Mom making so often. Even though it wasn't Italian, it was what he craved. That, and *only that* recipe, would satisfy.

"Tell me again how you roast a chicken."

"Dad, it's nine p.m. You're cooking? At this hour?"

"What else do I have to do?"

It was late. I was tired. I had just finished a long conversation with Son #1 and a second one with Son #2. Both were

away at college struggling with relationship and laundry is-
sues. Even JB, lying at my feet, was giving me a look that had
an agenda.

I sighed. "Okay. Ready? Got a pencil?"

HE HUNG THE PHONE in its cradle, ambulated with his cane to
the refrigerator, recipe in hand, and removed the bird. He un-
wrapped it and placed it in the v-shaped roasting rack he had
received by mail order just that afternoon. The accompanying
brochure guaranteed chicken roasted on this rack to be as juicy
and tender as he remembered.

He set the chicken on the rack and placed it on top of
the stove. The oven clock read nine thirty, a little late to cook.
Maybe he'd use the microwave instead of the oven to save time.
He maneuvered, then precariously placed the rack next to the
microwave door. The rack with the chicken on it was too big to
fit inside. *On to the oven.*

He opened the oven door. Pots and pans. He had never
actually *used* the oven for baking. After removing and stacking
the pots and pans in the sink, he put the bird in the pre-
heated oven.

Three quarters of an hour later, the heady aroma of roasting meat filled the apartment. His mouth watered. The rack
worked! He could already taste his succulent meal.

He bent down with one hand on his cane. With the other,
he reached for the oven door. He opened it, pulling it all the
way down, and reached for the rack nesting the bird. As he
lifted the rack from the oven, he felt his center of gravity shift.
The rack listed to the right. Makings for the golden gravy (the

natural juices that the brochure instructed him would self-baste the bird to perfection) spilled onto the bottom of the oven. He shifted to right himself and adjust his balance.

Zip! The chicken sailed across the kitchen floor. At the same time the natural juices ignited a grease fire in the oven, triggering the smoke alarm in his apartment. That alarm automatically set off multiple alarms throughout the entire wing of his building, prompting forty elderly ladies to pour out of their apartments in various states of lounge wear. Several of them were reportedly screaming.

The security guard arrived and herded everyone back to their apartments. "Okay, everyone, no harm done."

"Well, it seems you're doing a little late night cooking again, eh, John?" The guard was kind enough to assist my father with cleaning up his kitchen: the oven blackened, the floor dangerously slick with grease, the chicken flattened. It seemed that the bird had been stepped on once by my father as he tried to regain his balance (a maneuver he had perfected on all those cruise ships). It had been trampled a second time by a neighbor with early-stage Alzheimer's who thought she was stomping on a large rat.

At Sunday dinner in my home after church, I asked: "How did the chicken come out, Dad?"

"Perfect," he said quietly.

"JUST GET ME OUT OF HERE."

"Dad, the doctors want you to. . . ."

"I don't care what the doctors say. I'm going to die, but not in this bed in this place. I'm going home."

"Really, Dad. It's impossible for you to stay in your apartment. You must be ambulatory. *Ambulatory.*" He had lost weight in the hospital, developed complications from surgery and now needed assistance with his daily activities. He had managed the transition well from his independent apartment to a smaller one in the assisted living center, but *this*. This series of complications made me wonder if he could return to his apartment.

He glared at me, his mind already fixed on the decision. I knew I would never win. "Make this happen. Make it happen today," he barked.

He and I both knew the prostate cancer had spread and left him no further options. My frustration was mixed with a tinge of sympathy for this man lying shriveled and gray in his own pajamas in the hospital bed. He had refused to wear a hospital gown, "Makes me feel like a girl. Makes me feel *stupido*." *Stupido*, the word his mother had used when she was frustrated.

I STOOD AT THE END of his hospital bed, his first born, remembering it all. There was nothing he had asked of me that was easy. He had wanted me to be a math prodigy when that was the most difficult subject for me. I spent Monday through Thursday evenings in tears at the dining room table as he tutored me in math. With his help I got a solid C minus. In the late sixties I cut my hair in a pixie cut, loving freedom from permanents and wearing curlers to bed every night. He was horrified and made me wear a hat as I rode in the backseat of the Chevy so he didn't have to look at it. By the time I was sixteen, it was boys. He didn't approve of a single boyfriend. "Not college material. Surely you can do better." I was convinced that nothing I did would please him. *Not Enough.*

I LOOKED AGAIN AND SAW how diminished he was. I knew that the rest of his life would be about small victories, things he could control, like where he died. When his charm and the cruise clothes and his awards were all stripped away, what was left? An old guy who needed just as much love as he did when he was younger. Maybe more. *Maybe much more.*

"I guess we could see about getting you twenty-four-hour care at the assisted living center."

"Just do it. Whatever it costs. I'll pay."

So that is how he spent the last weeks of his life. A hospital bed was rolled into the living room of his apartment. He was surrounded by Mom's paintings, Eddie Arnold ballads, and three local mountain women, who each kissed him goodbye at their end of their shift. Daily visits from his current girlfriend were scheduled when he was most alert and in freshly ironed pajamas. He died four weeks after he left the hospital, *at home.*

His memorial service was held in the retirement center auditorium. As I spoke of his life, I looked down from the lectern into that first row of heartsick women, all sobbing, their lacy, white handkerchiefs waving like flags as he cast off on his next journey.

THE HOLLOW SCOOPED OUT in the gravel between my parents' side-by-side graves is new, well-defined, bowl shaped, and centered an equal distance between them. The depression is there for a purpose. I know by now to pay attention to the changes I see at Sweet Woods Garden, no matter how puzzling. Gravel around the other graves is smooth, undisturbed. Are my parents, John's grandparents, creating a bowl in which to hold his pain? Carry it? Hold mine? *Never mind who is to benefit. I accept this gift and pray that I will stay malleable, molding to the will of the five souls lying here who are wiser than I.*

All around me I see change. The yellow quince drops its bitter fruit, leaving food for the deer. The dogwood is full of red berries, and a wood thrush finds the fruit an easy reach. He is usually shy, but today he is busy gorging himself and ignores me. His flute-like song echoes his discovery of such abundance.

I hear the rustle of wings above my head, softer than a bird. Dragonflies. *I stand still, extend my arm, and a dragonfly lights on my outstretched finger. Her slender black legs cling to it, nearly encircling it. She is probing with her long abdominal segment, lifting and dipping her tail up and down on my finger. Is she testing for ownership, staking me out to see if I am a mate? I feel her hard nose probe my finger and I am startled by the strength of her grasp.* Such tenacity. *Strangely, the distraction of the insect keeps me focused on this place and the role I play in it.*

The voices here call for change, *not my favorite word. Change sends a shudder of apprehension through me and I feel my body stiffen, resist, forgetting my prayer for malleability. I prefer the routine, the familiar, but then I am in the wrong place for that.*

I sit on the stone bench I had made, a slab of thick cement balanced on a base of river rock. A small brass marker set into the cement seat reads, "King of the Hill," a nickname given to Henry by our neighbors. They watched him work at the table and single chair he had set up at the highest point on our property with the panorama of the Blue Ridge Mountains behind him. He sat there with his Wall Street Journal, *cell phone, and red briefcase, sorting paperwork for the company he still ran long distance by phone. I bet the marker makes him grin.*

As I sit on the bench today I notice the surface is pitted with fifteen years of North Carolina winters, ice storms, heavy summer rains, mountain sun, and may provide a nocturnal resting spot for a raccoon or two.

This is the place I sit and contemplate John's journey, the one that has taken him to China. My Not Enough wisdom has sent him to a place where the doctors will stimulate the stagnated neurons in the blocked channels of his body to make them flow again. He has gone to save his life, to find his life. The nurses there are caring for him and he wants to believe in the treatment. Trust it, my heart.

Through Skype, John says that his physician, Doctor Lo, tells him corny jokes in broken English every day at the end of treatment. He has instructed John that he must learn to laugh again, "Heal the brain, heal the body." He flashes a toothy grin as his white coat disappears out the door, John tells me.

John is no longer using a cane or wearing a boot. He has met other Americans who are there for treatment of neurological diseases, Parkinson's, stroke, multiple sclerosis, and made new friends. They have reduced his medications from twelve to six. Maybe, just maybe, I'll get my son back.

The crape myrtle tree near my left shoulder has grown tall enough to meet the dogwood by my right side, forming a canopy above my head. The crape myrtle is in bloom and its fuchsia flowers add their colorful accent to the Carolina-blue sky. The gray slate walkway at my feet is moldy, covered with azaleas that keep it dark and moist. Everything here defies horticulture, is overgrown, makes its own rules. I look up and feel hugged tight, encircled by green. "Snug," Mom called it. A feeling of satisfaction coats the back of my mouth. I swallow it whole.

Now that John is in China, I have been spending more time here, needing the energy of the garden to fortify me. John will need *it, too. I tell him, "Believe in the garden." There is a pause in our conversation and I do not think it is the Skype connection. Maybe he has his hands full dealing with being away and having six hours of treatment six days a week, acupuncture, tuina, a form of Chinese massage he loves (before he left for China, no therapist could touch him near his foot for fear of setting off waves of pain), physical therapy, and traditional Chinese medicine not to mention learning the language and the customs of the culture. So I say, "Okay, honey. I'll believe in the garden for both of us. We're all pulling for you." "Okay, Mom," he says, "gotta go."*

Between dawn and mid-morning a haze settles low near the ground and it almost appears that the line between the sky and the ground disappears. I live in Transylvania County and the light during this time of day is a perfect backdrop for a vampire film. But I have my very own ghosts.

By late morning the sky is clear, but the mountain ridges beyond are still hazy. Monarch butterflies and tiger swallowtails light on the grass at the top of the hill drinking lingering drops of dew.

Wild birds forage in the thicket next to the cemetery. Redbirds, bluebirds, and indigo buntings feed on dropped wildflower seeds. I have intentionally allowed these flowers to re-seed and grow uncut to keep the birds happy, thriving. Every so often a hummingbird zips from her tiny nest hidden in the forest beyond to feed on nectar I have placed in my feeder in my front yard. Bees thrive, buzzing happily while pollinating wildflowers. At dusk the temperature drops. Just as the sun begins to sink, bats swarm above the beech trees and nosedive, feeding on insects during the last moments of light. Moments later the sun falls into the mountains. Night descends, black as death. Nothing vanishes. Nothing.

*S*he is not unlike a big-chested woman, arms outstretched, reaching to gather children to her bosom, this city Tianjin. I peeked from behind her skirts and watched the noisy chatter of taxis scurrying, bicycles whirring. The traffic light, a long red, allowed me to watch all seven lanes of cars, trucks, buses, vans, bicycles and pedestrians sprint past on their way to work, to school, to shop or forage in this city that is her home. Her world was no small realm and so different from the tiny mountain town I had left to travel there. Yet the disparity between my North Carolina home and this place didn't trouble me. Rather, I was strangely comfortable in this bustling city where so many abided in harmony and swayed in perfect rhythm like well-matched dancers.

The light turned green, yellow and back to red. Still, I didn't cross. I stood at the edge of the curb, a captive of this city's verve. I was charmed by the bustle and show around me. Thousands of Mother Tianjin's children passed by. I shook my head and wondered how she managed all her charges in this orderly, melodic dance.

Once again, the light changed. I crossed seven lanes of traffic, slipping into the flow without a hitch. I heard the whir of wings above as I crossed. *Dragonflies.* All the while the song in my head played over and over: *"Nothing vanishes. Nothing vanishes. Nothing."* Hundreds of dragonflies followed, chaperoning me. These gossamer-winged companions, the souls of the dead, the brothers and sisters of the dragonflies that followed me to my family cemetery at the top of the hill in North Carolina were there. I marveled that I was halfway around the world in a strange, new city, alone, yet this place was familiar, filled with what comforted me.

John has been in China six weeks in this city full of strangers. He had achieved full range of motion in his left foot, the one that was frozen in place when he arrived.

I was in China for a ten-day visit. I felt a kinship with these people who had nurtured my son, and who I was certain would restore his health. I followed the narrow footpath along the sidewalk past the rows and rows of hundreds of bicycles parked in front of the hospital and stopped at the statue there. The twenty-foot marble figure looked down at me. Huang Ti, the Yellow Emperor and philosophical founder of Traditional Chinese Medicine, pure white marble in a long robe.

All around me people were hurrying, with taxis pulling in and out of the entrance to this twelve-hundred bed, thirteen-story hospital. Noises faded, save spinning wings above. Huang Ti's eyes spoke to me: *"You have chosen wisely to come to this place."*

The cemetery on top of the hill where the five lie and speak to me reminded me: *Nothing Vanishes*. These two worlds converged, my vision shifted. I was altered by it forever.

I stood in the presence of memory I could not see, but felt, a presence of past healing and hope for myself, for my son. The hope of the other patients I would see that day was embodied in this tall slab of marble. *Nothing vanishes. Nothing.*

Chinese women passed me and saw me acting so unlike the rest of the throng racing by. The rest of the crowd was fast-paced, focused on a destination. I was a casual, slow-moving observer caught up in the details: a colorful scarf, a newsboy's cap, a pair of miniscule, red, American-made high heels on the tiny feet of a young Chinese woman riding a bicycle.

A tiny, blue taxi screeched to a halt at my feet. Two young men leaped from the rear doors and raced toward the front of the cab where an old woman was sitting. She remained still, apparently unaffected by the commotion around her. One of the young men opened the passenger door, while the second got on his hands and knees next to the door, placing his body as close to the car as possible. The woman was gently lifted from the cab by the second man. She was rolled onto the back of the kneeling man and locked her arms around his neck. He stood and carried this tiny, withered woman, no bigger than a ten-year-old child, up the six steps to the hospital entrance. This frail Chinese woman was probably the revered elder in her family. These young men would consider it a loss of face to allow her to walk those six steps unaided, alone.

It was nearly nine o'clock in the morning. Throngs of people climbed the steps to the entrance. Outpatients had been arriving since four-thirty. The hospital staff would treat 6000 outpatients that day. Chinese patients were busy finding their places in line for treatment and no one took time to watch this tender moment with me. I witnessed it alone.

This moment reminded me of all the times I had driven past the nursing home in my hometown and waved to the young man sitting alone in a wheelchair, facing the passing traffic and waving to anyone, *anyone at all,* who bothered to notice him. The anonymous occupants of those cars were his family, his life, his world.

I could hear my favorite aunt, Mimi, cluck her tongue. This old Italian who never left her mother's home had taught me the strength and love of family. Her voice was sharp and clear, *"Shame on them for not visiting that young man. Look at the Chinese, the ones my youngest brother Geno called 'those damn Commies.'* They understand family, just like us Italians." I see her settle back into herself and relax the long body she leaned forward when she wanted attention. Her tongue stopped cluck-ing, her breathing relaxed, and her image faded.

THERE WAS MUCH CONVERSATION between the two men as they maneuvered "Grandmother" (as I decided to call her) through the hospital entrance toward a wheelchair. Their movements were so simple and fluid I knew they had done it often. Their loud Chinese chatter crackled around this old lady, yet she re-mained unruffled in her plain, beige housecoat.

Once inside they would join others without appointments in the outpatient line. They would wait until a doctor saw them and treated Grandmother with acupuncture, moxibus-tion, a ginseng soak, or whatever would heal her. They would probably be at the hospital all day, and then spend most of the evening traveling, going back to their province unless they were fortunate enough to have family living in Tianjin with whom they could stay. If the doctor decided that Grandmoth-er was sick enough to be admitted to the hospital, select fam-ily members would stay in her room and sleep on the floor at the foot of her bed. Her family would ensure that she had tea in the morning and would wash her clothes, feed her home-cooked meals of rice rolls and healing soups, and bathe her. Even though there were plenty of nurses on the floor to help, it would be considered loss of face to allow anyone outside the family to care for a sick family member. And, no one in the province where she lives would know she was there. This is *family business*, a private matter. I grinned as I imagined my aunt's delight over the shared values between the Italians and the "Communists."

I walked through the corridors past the pharmacy. The scent of ginseng, garlic and unfamiliar herbs filled my head. Passing through the first building, I stepped into an open area with a walkway under construction to connect the three hospital buildings into one giant complex. Hospital employees noted my Western dress. "*Ninhâo*," I said, and smiled. Nearly always, I received a hello and smile in return.

Dragonflies flickered above my head as hospital workers swept the floor with handmade bamboo brooms, raising dust. The dragonflies buzzed and darted, continuing to chaperon me. These old, adaptive creatures, like this ancient culture, have created their own rules for survival. They appeared motionless as they hovered, suspended, their bodies defying gravity, reminding me of the Tai Chi movements of the Chinese men and women exercising early in the morning on the street and in the park. I passed into the connecting buildings and walked toward the elevator that would take me to the twelfth floor to visit John.

I smelled the scent of orchids and fresh lilies and other pungent exotic flowers as I lingered in the hallway next to the newly renovated cafeteria. The scent came from the six-foot, bamboo frame threaded throughout with hundreds of freshly cut flowers. Several days before, on one of my walks through the neighborhood near my apartment, I had watched women fill these frames with flowers in front of a flower shop. Once decorated, they were loaded onto carts drawn by bicycles and delivered FTD China style only better, cheaper, and more spectacular than at home. With flowers and fireworks, the Chinese celebrate business openings and births and honor their dead. In this city of fifteen million, I heard bursts of fireworks several times throughout the day and night and saw women on bicycles pedaling along with these tall, colorful arrangements, weaving a splash of color among the endless lanes of traffic.

Today I carried a few Yuan along with a note written in Chinese. I had been instructed by my host, the medical director of the program in which John was a client, to pick up a box of acupuncture needles. I approached a small stand with a glass-enclosed display case where the hospital sold acupuncture needles. The woman attendant read my note, bowed to me, reached into the glass case, and selected a box of the appropriately sized needles. The box was placed in front of me for inspection. When I approved, I received a slight bow and the exchange occurred. She smiled at me, dropping her eyes. I handed her the Yuan and she returned change.

Even though this was business, I felt acknowledged, *important*. No slipping of credit cards through a machine. Her deference to me said *I am not worthy* in the most formal sense that is Chinese. I felt humbled by these simple unspoken rules of this ancient culture, honoring another person even in a simple exchange of goods. When she presented the box I felt as if I had received a gift. I walked to the elevator, the needles humming their healing song inside my shoulder bag. My head was filled once again with the scent of star-gazer lilies, bird of paradise, Fiji mums.

Hospital elevators there are old by Western standards. There were just two in this wing, so the line of patients, family members, and staff swelled as we watched the floor numbers – five, four, three – flash above the elevator doors. The waiting group shifted back and forth. People moved between the two elevators watching the numbers, each jockeying for the best spot when the door opened. The group crowded forward, eager to board so they wouldn't have to wait for another round.

The doors opened and a tightly packed group uncoiled, stepped off and filed out. Those of us in the front of the line piled in. The elevator operators were all women and they slid out with the departing group to make way for the ascending group.

As soon as the operator closed the door, we called out our floors. "*Shièr* (twelve)," I said. Then, almost always, a warning bell signaled an unbalanced load. The operator opened the door. She selected specific riders to step off, then on, arranging passengers to stand in a *slightly* different spot on the floor. We were jostled with the shuffling of feet. She smiled, ready to ascend, and perched her tiny frame on a three-legged stool next to the controls. Audible sighs of relief filtered throughout.

We stopped on nearly every floor on the way up. Wheelchairs, patients in metal hospital beds, and a pharmacy cart stacked with bamboo baskets of prescription-ground herbs piled in rice paper stacks replaced passengers who stepped off, competing for tiny, postage-stamp size space. At least twice more during the ascent we got off and on to re-balance the load.

By this time everyone on the elevator was late, delaying scheduled appointments, but no one minded. There, everything takes as long as it takes, and in spite of an elevator that ran on its own timetable and long lines everywhere, patients received treatment. Not a single soul around me had the harried look of an American. No one there forgot to breathe. No one there forgot his place or misread how important it was not to press the button for his floor, but to allow the elevator operator to do her job.

The elevator groaned upward. Families with giant laundry bags (possibly clean clothes for a family member) and employees carrying their lunch for the day, a two-quart, clear glass jar of water infused with tea leaves settling on the bottom and a small package of sticky rice balls, stepped on.

I reached the twelfth floor and squeezed out of my allotted space. I saw nurses in crisp white uniforms, their skirts standing away from their slender frames like open umbrellas. Each time I entered the twelfth floor, I ran my fingers across the raised print on the bracelet on my left arm: "Believe in miracles." It was a gift I had bought to honor my son's healing. I almost never removed it. Silly, I know. Unlike me, usually so practical, but somehow this lucky piece felt right. The bracelet glistened in the sunlight, carrying hope and the promise of John's recovery as I opened the door to 1203.

Nothing vanishes. Nothing.

I knew Elna would return to Grandma's home. The pull was too great, no matter how much she had yearned to walk down the steps of that gray frame house and out the door. She belonged there. I knew she would always return to her place at the table between Ma and her sister Mimi. The triad seemed inseparable. I often thought of them as one. "Grandma, Mimi and Elna," rolled off my tongue like one word. They were used to living together, twenty-four hours a day, sharing the apartment on the second floor. Elna belonged there just as much as Grandma's gold damask wing chair that sat in the living room next to the ever-blooming violets.

Elna's short marriage seemed like some sort of vacation to an exotic island where she had gotten too much sun and her skin had burned; where the food hadn't agreed with her; and where she had stayed up too late, feeling logy the next day. Home was where she belonged.

ELNA ELIZABETH CARRARO OPENED the same front door of the same two-story house at 12035 Normal Avenue and reluctantly climbed the same sixteen steps as she had done for twenty years. Her battered, brown, pressed-cardboard suitcase bumped behind her, rhythmically marking her hesitant footsteps. Climbing the steps today made her legs ache. A knot formed in one calf. She stopped, reached down, rubbed the sore spot and frowned.

She was certain, just three months before (when she left carrying the same suitcase down those sixteen steps) that she would return to visit for Sunday dinner with a different last name, a husband, and a stepson. That didn't happen. Today she returned home more alone than ever, knowing that, as much as she denied it, this house defined her.

The landing led to the hallway that served as the entrance to the second floor apartment. Mittens, the gray and black family terrier, raced from his place under the mahogany dining room table to greet her. "Mittens, sweet boy!" Elna bent forward to pet him as he pawed her legs, his white-mitten feet clamoring for attention. Elna felt the familiar softness of his fur and petted him a second time. "I'm glad to see you, too." Tears filled her dark eyes. She wiped them away. The string of multicolor beads resting on her ample 44DDD chest had swung forward, then bounced back on their shelf as she stood. (No matter what, she was never without her "junk jewelry," as she called it.)

She exhaled a deep sigh. Looking into the terrier's soft brown eyes, she said, "Well, guess I'd best not cry over spilled milk." She straightened and fingered her beads, "We'll save that for the cat, Yang, eh?" She laughed at her own small joke.

Mittens followed her into the bedroom. Elna set her suitcase on the throw rug next to the same mahogany twin bed she had slept in alone for twenty years. "Never thought that," fanning the space above the headboard, "could look so appealing." Mittens sat on the edge of the throw rug and watched her attentively. She brushed a speck of lint from her spotless pink chenille bedspread.

She stood and turned to leave the room. Ma greeted her at the door, "So, you back now?"

"Yeah, Ma."

"So life over there no good, eh?"

"Frank was different than I thought." Elna dropped her chin and stared at the oak floorboards in the doorway. *The floor needs waxing, dusting.* She raised her eyes to meet her mother. "Different. He wasn't who I thought he was."

"They never are. Never." Ma was silent a moment. "You be with *la famiglia*, eh? You brothers, sisters. They glad to see you. Johnny help you with *legale* and *annullamento*. I no know about *prete* (the priest). I say many *rosarios* for you." Ma wiped her hands on her apron, reached out and petted Elna's arm. Elna watched her mother thump toward the kitchen in men's gray woolen house slippers with flattened backs. *She needs new house slippers.*

The familiar smells of *Cornetti* rolls baking in the oven penetrated the warm August air in the apartment. The yeasty buttery scent left a comforting, familiar aroma. Elna could already see the brown topknots on the fat pillows of dough. She pictured Ma dissolving the yeast in water and adding salt, sugar, milk and shortening to a mound of semolina flour in the center of the white enamel utility table in the middle of the kitchen. She could see Ma's hands kneading, punching down, turning, again kneading and punching down the dough, and then plopping it in the large green bowl for a final rising.

All her life *pane*, bread, had graced her mother's table. *Pane*, nourishment, grist for the day. She never had been truly hungry at home. Oh, they had been through lean times. During the Great Depression everyone in the family was out of work except her brother Johnny. When he found out that his job was being eliminated, he told his boss that he would be responsible for putting eight people on the street. So he kept his job and the family paid the mortgage with his salary, although they had to eat a lot of spaghetti, *pane*, dandelion greens picked from the yard, and *"zuppa,"* soup, (as Ma called it).

But the hunger Elna felt today was different. She had left the house to marry at forty-nine, searching for something more than *pane*. She craved happiness with this man Frank. But Frank could not provide sustenance. He could not give her what she needed because he did not know it in his own life. His table was bare. His bread dry and tasteless.

"Matrimonio insipido." Elna plopped herself on her bed and smoothed the nubby fabric of her wool skirt with her ring-less fingers.

"WHEN SHE LAUGHS, she brings us all together, you know?" Eda, nodded to Mary and they watched their sister Elna slide right back into her role as hostess the following Sunday afternoon. Elna mixed Manhattans and passed a plate of canapés around the living room. "Did I tell you the one about. . . ?" Elna began another of her series of jokes and one-liners. She was always the first to laugh at her own gags.

"Especially with all she has been through," the youngest sister, Olga, chimed in, wiping her eyes with the lace handkerchief she kept tucked in her sleeve.

"Oh, that!" Eda snorted. "That was just good judgment,

coming back here to be with the people who *really* love her. I'm proud of my sister for doing it. I don't care what Ma says about the church, the annulment, or the priest. She deserves happiness." Eda was the quietest of the sisters and this statement surprised the others. They looked up from their handwork, then nodded in agreement. "And, I've missed her experiments."

The experiments had been part of Elna's ongoing efforts to learn to cook. Ma controlled the kitchen by doing all the cooking, and sometimes it seemed to the two sisters still living at home, that it was a way of keeping them there, dependent on her. Each Saturday Elna watched television chef Graham Kerr's program, "The Galloping Gourmet." Elna became an avid fan. Graham told jokes while he prepared recipes and seemed like the kind of man Elna wished Frank had been. Graham sped back and forth across the kitchen set dressed in a tux or three-piece suit, trim and fit, preparing meals with copious amounts of butter and cream while sloshing down glass after glass of wine from a fine crystal goblet. He'd laugh when his soufflé would not rise, the sauce curdled, or a pan full of browning onions filled the test kitchen with smoke.

That Sunday, Elna was wearing her standard black slacks. Self-conscious about her stick-thin legs, she kept them covered. On her feet were black, tied, serviceable shoes that allowed room for her bunions and hammertoes. A red sweater added a punch of color. Black button earrings matched the black beads that swung from her neck as she moved around the family circle serving appetizers. A whiff of Coty Air-Spun Powder lingered behind her. With a free hand she fluffed her new perm and said to her sister-in-law, Maribel: "These curls are still so tight I feel like a poodle. Hope Mittens doesn't get feisty with me." Elna's beads danced across her chest as she and Maribel giggled.

"Mal, is the salad ready?" Elna called to her sister by her given name, Malya (my cousins and I called her "Mimi"). Recently released from a long hospitalization for depression, Mimi moved slowly. Elna, the middle child and peacemaker, tried to prompt Mimi before Ma's shrill, demanding voice caused conflict. She peeked around the corner of the kitchen to see Mimi cutting bright red tomato chunks into a bowl of greens. The juice from the tomatoes dripped into the bowl, Mimi's secret to giving the olive oil and balsamic vinegar dressing just the right tang.

Carrying the empty canapé plate into the kitchen, Elna saw me at the table next to Mimi munching on the end of a sliver of *Asiago* cheese: "So you're the little mouse in our kitchen today, eating that last bit of cheese." Ma stood with her back to Elna at the stove stirring polenta counter clockwise, believing that if she stirred it only in one direction while she cooked it, *malocchio*, the evil eye, could not be cast upon her family.

After dinner, the women gathered in a circle in the living room, tatting. They whispered behind their hands. *Secrets.* Like who was going through early menopause, whose husband drank too much, and who had a doctor's appointment for an undisclosed illness.

"Come, come, come in!" Elna ushered me and my cousin Judy into her bedroom, a room where lace curtains hung at the single window. She reached into the top drawer of the antique dresser that she had picked up at a neighborhood garage sale and refinished. She lifted out the white Fannie Mae candy box that she had découpaged with bright flower cutouts and pulled off the cover. "Pick one." Inside the box lay a jumble of mismatched earrings, every color of the rainbow. "Now, that one, Judy," she pointed to the single earring my younger cousin selected, "has a missing stone, but I think it's pretty anyway."

I selected a red plastic, drop earring. Looking over Elna's shoulder, I eyed her twin boudoir, milk-glass lamps with pink lace shades on the dresser. The lamps were another garage sale find. Her collection of necklaces draped the lampshades. After Judy and I picked our single earrings, Elna replaced the lid and returned the box to the drawer that held rows and rows of matched earrings stored in open egg cartons. She looked at us both clutching our treasures, "I always feel better when I've got a little something sparkly to wear, don't you?"

THE TELEPHONE RANG. And rang again. Neither Elna nor Mimi picked it up. Both sisters looked at each other briefly before returning their steady gaze to the screen. Neither sister left her place in front of the television.

"I can't believe it! Erica's going to have an abortion!" Mimi gasped.

"Shh." Elna's sandwich hung between her fingers in mid-air while she watched their favorite soap opera.

Whoever was calling wasn't family. *La famiglia* knew better than to call at this hour. Even the priest knew. This was the one hour each day, five days a week, that they watched the soaps, "The Young and the Restless" and "All My Children." This ritual, along with "The Galloping Gourmet" on Saturday, weekly forages to bargain at neighborhood garage sales, and attendance at Mass filled their days after they retired as clerks from the Illinois Central Railroad. Sundays were set aside to help Ma with the family dinner.

Their obsession with the soaps was more of a mental-health break than anything else. While many family members believed it was the soaps that gave the spinster aunts insights into marriage and family life, the sisters knew differently. They lived complex lives, filled with as much stress as the characters they watched on television.

They had lived through Elna's divorce (and a church annulment), Mimi's long-term hospitalization for chronic depression in a state mental hospital, and before that, her stay in a tuberculosis sanitarium and surgery for the removal of one lung. Their oldest brother, who lived on the first floor of the two-flat, suffered from depression so severe that he had been given electro-convulsive therapy. Six blocks away, the oldest sister lived with manic-depressive illness and was either in her cups or petitioning Mayor Daley's office for political reform. Their father had died of stomach cancer and their mother was aging badly. A niece had become pregnant out of wedlock. On top of it all, they knew, *they just knew*, that a favorite sister-in-law, living twenty-five minutes away, was terribly unhappy in her marriage to their brother Johnny, but they just couldn't put their finger on *why*.

The soaps were their respite, a time when they could watch the drama unfold and bear no responsibility for the outcome. At the end of the hour they snapped off the television: "Okay, back to our chores." Each sister would select a single Fannie Mae chocolate from the shiny, white, gift box (their preferences were cremes, easier on dental bridges than caramels and nuts), replace the lid and place the box in a drawer until the following day.

Saturday afternoon before the five o'clock mass, house slippers were put away and sturdy shoes and loose clothes were donned for serious garage-sale hunting. Elna and Mimi collected pressed glass, milk glass, and carnival glass, paying fifty cents, sometimes a dollar, sometimes as much as five dollars for an iridescent powder box of carnival glass or a footed glass compote. Cup hangers were added inside to the glass fronted mahogany secretary (a garage-sale find) in the living room to hold demitasse cups. "Our treasures," they said. Elna beamed as Mimi poured over books they collected to learn how to read the markings on the backs of china and glassware.

Over the years their treasures increased in value. The investments they made with the profit from selling them provided funds to build a retirement home in Arkansas. It was next to family land owned by a brother-in-law in a small community of Italians called Little Italy. They had saved enough to pay for the cost of the land and the house with more than enough left to provide for both of them for the next thirty years.

When they died there was still a balance that became, at their request, an educational trust to be used by *la famiglia* to assist their beloved nieces and nephews and their children. The trust was administered by a childless, married nephew. "He will be fair," they said.

These were two smart, little old ladies who spent their working lives as simple clerks in the Illinois Central Railroad accounting office. They took what they learned and made it benefit those they loved.

ELNA ROSE FROM THE TWIN BED to find one of the many Shih
Tzus (all called "Precious") that had replaced Mittens at her
feet. She snapped on a floral housecoat, slipped into scuffs and
let the dog out near the fig tree that bordered her property in
Arkansas. She returned to her bedside table and picked up a
caplet, a small bracelet-sized rosary which she slid on her wrist,
unconsciously tapping the last black bead that hung from its
silver cross, a daily ritual. *"Always a prayer for the ones gone before us."* She told the women at the Altar Guild that the wrist
rosary was easier to manage than a standard, longer rosary.
"Speed dialing," she called it, and the women around the table
laughed, some behind their hands, but her good friend Mary
Vero belly-laughed along with Elna.

She plugged in the battered six-cup Farberware percolator
she had set up the night before and watched as the brown liq-
uid darkened the glass top. The fragrant smell of morning coffee filled the kitchen. Her pot was legendary, the only one she
ever used. "I like my coffee hot. Hot. Not that lukewarm stuff
that comes from those lousy Mr. Coffee makers." She didn't
have a morning appetite. Never did.

She was rarely hungry these days. Her stomach was always sour. She hoped her cancer would not recur like Pa's and
Mary's as stomach cancer. Elna ran her hands through her head
of short salt and pepper curls, "Guess I'll need another perm
soon." Precious looked up at her as she thought about driving
the black Ford sedan down the two-lane road with no shoulder
and sitting in the two-seat beauty shop with county women
she didn't know. She reconsidered, "Maybe I can get another
couple of weeks out of it."

She handed Precious a dog biscuit and opened the tin
of butterhorns she'd baked yesterday. Their buttery promise

stirred her appetite. She removed two and set them on a fine china plate to eat with her coffee. She thought about how her sister would prepare hot oatmeal with fresh milk and raisins and look virtuous. "Oh, the hell with it." She lifted one butterhorn and thought about Graham Kerr's irreverent delight in eating whatever pleased him. "To the finer things!" She saluted the day with the cookie.

IN 1996, WHEN THEY WERE in their nineties, Elna traveled with her sisters to a family reunion in North Carolina. The trip was challenging – ten hours by car because Mimi was agoraphobic, had never flown and wouldn't consider it. Elna, Mimi, and Eda spent the trip wedged in the back seat of a nephew's car, screaming their way across the mountain ridges. Once they arrived, Mimi declared, "That's it. We're staying."

I WATCH ELNA'S BODY SLOW, and as I do, mine relaxes, knowing it is her time. *She deserves it. She earned it with her loyalty and her laughter that made everyone feel that everything was alright. She has earned this peace. I want it for her, a death that comes with loving hands surrounding her, like the loving hands she placed on me as a child, always offering something of herself, wanting me to leave her house with something in hand, a little sparkly or a bag of butterhorns, something to comfort me.* Now I watch her leave her generous body and am grateful for the hard choices she made for all the right reasons. For love for *la famiglia*.

Her hand wraps around mine, as warm and comforting as my childhood memories. Moments later, her long, thin fingers begin to cool. I cradle her fingers in mine, capturing her last bit of vitality.

"I'm right here, Elna. It's okay. It's your turn to walk down the steps and out the door."

The room is full of evening shadows, quiet and mellow. She exhales a final time. I watch as her spirit leaves a body that she no longer needs. She floats toward the ceiling high above me, her body an empty vessel. Her spirit hovers there a few moments in a lingering farewell. Then, as if grabbed by an unseen hand, vanishes.

Mimi had learned to exist in the aftermath, living a life where, in the beginning, she really did believe in all the stuff about controlling one's destiny, about the way things fall, about *Chance, Fortune.* She had to drop out of high school after her sophomore year to help the family, working as a maid. She finished school at night. At seventeen, Malya was bright and well educated. She had read widely and believed in her ability to control her future. How many bad things could happen to a seventeen-year-old to make her question this belief?

She was lucky. She had not suffered much loss (at least, not of a family member), maybe a first love, but certainly not her innocence. She had not lived hard enough to feel dog-tired, bone-weary, whipped. She had not yet begun to understand that she was not in charge. She still believed in fate and philosophy and the strength of self-will. She had not been beaten down enough to be the injured party, everybody's fool in this world.

The tears she had shed were mostly for herself. She hadn't yet learned to cry for the world. That came later when she was in a dark corner holding her arms up in front of her face. *Then* she learned to be afraid of what was coming at her, of what she couldn't see, of what she couldn't control, of what she didn't know.

Malya Josephine Carraro, my aunt Mimi, gave me things, physical things that became containers for stories. She gave me (and each of her eighteen nieces and nephews) an afghan she had crocheted in wide zigzag patterns of multicolor yarn that provided an extra helping of warmth to stack at the foot of my bed. She made ravioli by hand, fat pillows of pasta rolled so thinly I could see the meat, spinach and ricotta filling through the dough. She cooked what she called *"grustolli"*, crisp, fried, sweet dough that she dropped in oil, then, as soon as it floated back to the top, removed it with a slotted spoon, piled it on a platter and sprinkled the delicate pastry with powdered sugar. One bite, and no matter how fastidious we were, none of us (not even my mother) could keep our faces, fingers or shirts free of the powdery stuff.

Mimi couldn't say "I love you" with words, so she made things. For years, it was Ma who stood over the four-burner stove stirring the yellow cornmeal to make polenta. Ma made the gravy, the veal roast on Sunday, and baked the *Cornetti* rolls, and cut ribbons of pasta with a long knife at the white enamel kitchen table. When Ma's legs got so bad she could no longer stand in the kitchen, it was Mimi who learned all the word-of-mouth ways of cooking from recipes that had never been written down. Success in the kitchen gave Mimi status in the family and earned her respect. Until then, her voice had been timid and hesitant. But now Mimi's voice was stronger, sometimes shrill and demanding: "Elna, watch that pot of ravioli. Don't let it get soft." She was the new matriarca.

As a child, I visited and stayed the weekend. Mimi took me into the kitchen and showed me how to make ravioli: pour a mound of semolina flour in the center of the table, make an indentation in the center, stir in salt, egg, olive oil, knead and roll out the dough until I can see the table top through it. There now, thin enough. Make a filling of chopped spinach, twice-ground pork and veal, and grated cheese. Cut into squares. Place a square of dough on the table, fill, top with another to cover the filling. Seal. Allow the pillows to rest.

I could not get the hang of the dough. "Too thick," Mimi's voice was sharp, critical. This was important, *it was love*, and food spoke for her. She prepared food in the way the Catholic Church had taught her to pray, each ingredient a petition: flour, gently poured, a source of strength, supplier of energy; egg, broken into the flour, a symbol of life and renewal; oil, green and thick to calm, pacify, lead a path to grace; salt, sprinkled, the zing, the underpinning of prayer.

My aunts fussed over simmering pots, muttering a running commentary about the outcome, their form of background music to cooking. "Get your butterhorns out on a nice plate for dessert," Mimi directed her sister. "Use that pressed-glass plate with the hobnail pattern from the shelf in the living room."

THE FAMILY SCENE WAS NOT much different after my aunts moved to Arkansas. I had driven thirteen hours from Chicago to Little Italy, Arkansas, to be with my aunts Elna and Mimi for a long weekend. I knew they had been cooking all week, and, like other family members who visited, I was expected to consume as much home-cooked food as possible. "Go to Little Italy for two days and gain five pounds," was the familiar story.

I walked into their house carrying a twelve-by-eighteen-inch box that I'd gift wrapped. I'd shopped the Fannie Mae seconds store, bagged #6 creme-filled chocolates and arranged the candies in rows between sheets of waxed paper. "My God!" Mimi exclaimed, "So much! We can't get them here, you know."

Of course, they *could* get them there, by mail order, but they were far too frugal to pay the shipping and handling charges on *candy*. The look on my aunts' faces was well worth the effort as they opened it. Then, after the exclamations and thanks, came *The Ritual*. The box was passed ceremoniously once around the table after a meal, then disappeared. When their company left, each of the two sisters would select a single piece to savor following lunch each day. They parceled out the candy this way until another family member came to visit and brought another box.

Mimi served us ravioli on an antique, oval, ceramic platter, one so large it took two hands to pass. A splash of gravy (homemade tomato sauce) and a handful of grated Asiago cheese topped ten to twelve ravioli laid on another stack of gravy and ravioli topped with cheese. By the time the platter went around the oval, oak dining room table once, it was empty. Twice more, Mimi stood at the stove, straining ravioli from the gently rolling water as the delicate pillows of dough rose to the top of the pot until we held up our hands, pleading, "No more! No more! *Sufficienza!*"

EVEN THOUGH MY CHILDHOOD HOME was just a half-hour drive from 12035 Normal Avenue, my grandmother and aunts lived in what seemed like a different world from us, especially when they went to church. The pews at St Catherine of Genoa Church, three blocks from Grandma's, offered little comfort, unlike those at the Ivanhoe Community Methodist Church my parents and I attended. The Methodist Ladies' Auxiliary raised funds to pay for seat pads for the walnut pews. The Catholics offered plain, oak benches for good reason. The Methodists who sat in the pews all around me, the Smiths, the Hawkins, and the Pearsons, all nodded off about halfway through the sermon, comfortable, padded and plumped. But the Catholics, the Constantinos, the Amatos, and the Crossers, were far too busy bouncing between kneeling benches and a hard pew to relax. With that constant up and down, with prayer and chanting. Well, how could one nap?

I saw the mystery of it all. The swinging orbs of incense that filled my nostrils, making them slightly itchy; the shadows thrown across my aunts' bowed heads as they prayed; the rainbow hues shining through the stained glass figures of Mary, Joseph, and Peter making the mass seem to me like a scene from a movie. The Latin was indecipherable. It was a mystical language yet my aunts knew all the signals, all the stops and starts of it. They were insiders in a world I did not understand. I longed to find the magical meaning in their beliefs.

My own experiences with church were as dry and dull as Reverend Schuler's bland, weekly messages, served like a poor excuse for salad, just celery sticks on a plain white plate. But the Catholics, *oh, the Catholics, they served it up right:* a wide, ceramic bowl with a hand-painted, purple eggplant pattern in the center, brimming with radicchio, mescalin, dandelion greens, ripe, red tomatoes, green peppers, and a salty hint of anchovy and shaved Parmesan cheese. I sat wide-eyed on a hard pew. *I'm Home. Home.*

MIMI SAT IN A SMALL, straight-backed mahogany chair with roses carved into the back of the frame. The chair was battered and wobbly when they bought it for several dollars at Mrs. Gobus' garage sale, a neighbor on Normal Avenue. Mimi needlepointed a new cover and Elna refinished the wood. The women in the family liked sitting on it when they came to dinner on Sunday. It was an ugly duckling made beautiful and useful and gave their working-class home a touch of elegance.

Today Mimi was sitting in the chair tatting to keep her hands focused and her mind occupied, to block out her ever-present depression. The spool of tatting thread lay on her lap, pure white against her drab mushroom-colored trousers. She picked up the tatting shuttle with one hand, held the thread in the other, and spun a lacy, spidery pattern for the center of the doily that would go on the armrest of Ma's chair. Again and again she looped the thread around her finger and pulled the shuttle through. In and out, in and out. Her fingers moved faster and faster.

But her mind refused to follow the rhythm of the tatting she had come to rely on to keep her focus. Another rhythm, discordant and jarring, was in her head. She moved her hands faster and faster. She shook her head back and forth. "No!" at first softly, then, "No!" louder. The voices crowded out all the space left inside her head. *Not Good Enough! Bad person! Failure! Slut! Bitch!* Terrible words, words she had never spoken out loud, formed in the front of her brain.

She tossed the tatting shuttle onto her lap next to the scissors she used to cut the thread. The lovely pewter scissors with scalloped carving on the handles were a find from last week's garage sale. They had cost just fifty cents. She remembered handing Mrs. Gobus two quarters. The money was new and shiny in her palm, much shinier than the scissors. Mrs. Gobus smiled. Mimi smiled. Each believed they got the best of the bargain. When Elna heard how little her sister had paid, she grinned, "So elegant and practical."

WITHOUT KNOWING HOW, Mimi finds the scissors in her hands with the sharp end pointed at her neck. Do it! Do it! Slut! DO IT! The voices grow louder and louder while her mind races with visions of columns of numbers. Mathematical calculations on small sheets of paper are flying around in her head – numbers written in pencil like the tabulations she had made at her desk at work. The desk she had sat behind appears among all the rows and rows of desks of the accounting department at the Illinois Central Railroad. Her desk is piled high with paper. She fears she will never finish in time to catch the five-fifteen train to go home with Elna today. She will be in this dark room all alone, unable to complete the work. Alone with the voices. Lost!

She feels her hand jerk and finds herself looking at the point of the scissors, at the blade, the sharp end. She looks around her at the living room and sees the beautiful, graceful, delicate patterns of the demitasse cups through the secretary's glass door – gold and blue, pink floral, lime green with oriental flowers – too beautiful, too graceful for this moment. She and her sister had collected all that delicate porcelain at tag sales and brought all that beauty into the house.

Then she sees her nieces and nephews standing over her body lying in her coffin, her bloody neck covered with pancake makeup that the undertaker uses to conceal the unguarded moment. A mortal sin. She will go to Hell.

She barely hears a voice calling her name, seemingly from a great distance.

"Aunt Mimi?"

"Aunt Mimi?" It was louder now.

"Grandma says she's making my favorite today, spaghetti." One of her nieces had come to the apartment from downstairs. She was staring open mouthed, wide-eyed at her aunt.

"Grandma!" she yelled. "Grandma! Mimi won't talk. She looks funny!"

Docelina Guadinnini Carraro came into the living room holding a long, wooden spoon in one hand, her bib apron tied over a gray house dress. "*Brutta notizia! Brutta notizia!* Bad news! Elna, call Johnny!" she commanded. Docelina pulled a rosary from her apron pocket, took the scissors from her silent daughter's raised hands, and draped the rosary over the fingers that held the scissors. The rosary slid from Mimi's hands as she reached for the tatting. She picked it up and slowly pulled the thread, tearing out the delicate pattern. The work unraveled.

"I couldn't. I just couldn't do it, Johnny."

"I don't think you have a choice, Mimi."

The two stared at each other for a moment. Silence was

unusual between them. Their home had always been filled with the noise and clatter of talk – siblings, parents, boarders – all competing in the crowded, second-floor apartment for air time on a jam-packed wavelength.

"We must follow your psychiatrist's suggestions if you want to continue your recovery, now that your hospitalization is over." Johnny reached out, gently putting his hand on his sister's shoulder, "We'll figure it out. Maribel is making a temporary bedroom in the sewing room at the top of the stairs. That way you'll have your own space and be close to our children. Since I will be traveling every week, it would be a great help to both of us."

"*Me?* Help *you?* In the condition I'm in?" Mimi folded her arms across her chest and pulled at the sleeves of her shapeless, gray sweater.

"You are better, you just can't go home yet. You heard what the psychiatrist said about you and Ma."

"I know."

"I know you can help with Karen. She's shy and the two of you seem to get on well, seem to understand each other."

Mimi's hands stopped fidgeting at the mention of Karen. How is it that she could feel this child's awkwardness around people, this child's discomfort? Neither she nor Karen ever seemed to fit in, but was it right for her to be caring for a child, for both children, after what she had seen, where she had been, and while she was still feeling fragile?

"So?" John leaned forward, waited.

"Oh, I don't know. I do feel close to the children, close to Maribel. She's like a *sorella*, a sister. And, I am glad to be here. If you think I can do it, I can try."

For the next several months and several summers afterward,

Mimi lived with us, helping Mom and joining us on family vacations. We went to family lodges, the kind that were popular in the 1950s and had names like "Evergreen Lodge" and "Twin Lakes" in upper Michigan and Wisconsin, with cabins, boat docks, a place to swim, and woods where blueberries were abundant.

I WAS TWELVE YEARS OLD and we were on vacation in Michigan at Twin Lakes. I bounded down the stairs of the cabin then stopped when I saw Aunt Mimi stretched out in a lounge chair lying in the sun. I stared at her napping, her head tilted up to catch the warmth of the afternoon sunshine. I was perplexed by this pose. Something was different here. I had always seen my aunt upright, composed, in a *chair*. Somehow it seemed as if I were watching something I was not supposed to see. She was loose in her body with her legs splayed and her arms relaxed with her palms up. I realized I had not seen my own mother or *any* adult woman at ease like this. Oh, I had caught a few glimpses when Mom watched "The Garry Moore Show" in the den in her pajamas, her face smeared with cold cream and her hair uncombed, sitting cross-legged on the sofa facing the TV. She would laugh at the crew-cut fellow who always wore a tiny, goofy bow tie.

But this. This just didn't fit my vision of grown-up women. It stood outside the narrow fence I had built around them. Until that day I had put them all behind a gate, fenced into living a life uncluttered by comfort with their own bodies.

I grinned with pleasure as I rambled around the grassy area where my aunt was lying, careful not to disturb her nap, her ease. I was wearing the yellow shorts Mom had made for me last month. I slipped my hands into my front pockets covered with appliquéd flowers that felt like two bulls' eyes over my thick, wide hips and thighs. Could I dare to lie in the sun stretched out like Aunt Mimi?

Paul streaked across the grass and squirted the back of my neck with his squirt gun. I tore after him with mine, sprinting from these thoughts back to childhood again.

"So how did school go today?"

"Okay." I was standing in a smocked dress that Mom had made, my scuffed Buster brown shoes toed inward. I stared at my feet and the ugly, sensible shoes Mom made me wear.

"Okay?" Mimi asked, placing her hand under my chin, lifting it to her eyes.

"Well, it's hard." I struggled to speak about the teasing that went on during recess, teasing about my shoes, my weight. *"Fatso, Tubby."*

How could Mom, my beautiful mother with her perfect figure, understand this? Mom possessed that magic ingredient we talked about in Girl Scout meetings, the goal of all girls, to be poised.

It was Mimi who understood. I felt as awkward in my gangly body as a baby struggling with its first steps and, like Mimi, I never seemed to be rid of rough edges, the bitten cuticles, too-curly hair, wrong shoes, socks or dress.

Mimi told me how, when she was not much older than I, before the family moved to Chicago, Grandma had sent her to work at the boss's home in Stambaugh, Michigan. Every day after school, she walked the three miles from the dirt roads of Caspian, where her family lived in a miner's company-owned house, a plain, wood shack, like all the others in the community, to the city to earn two dollars a week as a maid. The boss's house was a real home with two bathrooms, fine china, and a kitchen with a separate dining room. Each child had his own bedroom. The first weeks Mimi worked there, she had trouble not gawking at the size of the house, its spaciousness, all that *space* for just *one* family. How awkward she felt, pretending she knew what she was supposed to be doing in such a house! She had to get used to a clothes washing machine that plugged into the wall! It wasn't the same as Ma's tub on the back porch, with a hand-cranked ringer. After a while she got the hang of setting the table for dinner in the dining room with fancy silverware. Six pieces at each place with a large, square, linen napkin (that she had ironed) beside the silver.

My aunt knew that if she taught me some skill, especially something to do with my hands (rather than biting my nails down to my cuticles), that I would have a channel for all my worry and discomfort. "Come on, let's go into the den. I've got some odds and ends of yarn. I'll teach you the basic stitches of crochet."

I followed her to the den, no longer staring angrily at my shoes.

IT WAS AS IF SHE HAD DRAWN a self-circumscribed circle around herself in her nineties. She was still troubled by demons. I visited her daily, driving the few minutes from my home in North Carolina to the tiny apartment where my two aunts lived in the assisted living center. I always had something in hand like flow-ers, cookies, or fresh, hard rolls, keeping a tradition they had begun when I was child. I had never left their home without a sparkly piece of jewelry or a brown paper sack full of baked goodies.

My aunts had matching blue recliners side-by-side in their sitting room, the kind with electric motors that gave them a boost up, now that they were having difficulty standing without assistance. Each had a walker. Elna's cancer was weakening her, but Mimi seemed strengthened by living in the mountains and listening to classical and sacred music and her books on tape.

"The Nun and the Party Girl." I grin every time I think about it. A cousin had come up with the phrase to describe Mimi and Elna, whose differences were so pointed and clearly reflected in their separate bedrooms. Mimi, who had worked in the office at St. Catherine of Genoa grade school, loved being around nuns and had aspired to become one, but her petition was refused because of her history of depression. Mimi's room was like a cell, a twin bed covered with a brown wool blan-ket, a straight-backed chair, and a rosary on the dresser with a dried palm leaf tied into a cross from a Palm Sunday mass. A single crucifix hung on the wall above the dresser. Plain brown wooden Venetian blinds hung at the single window. The muted tones of the afghan folded at the foot of her bed provided the only hint of color in the room.

Elna's room, all pink fluff and lace, had a soft, scatter rug on the floor next to her bed. On it were pink house slippers, ready to slide into when she rose each morning to make coffee. Mul-ticolor necklaces decorated the lace shades on the milk-glass, boudoir lamps on her dresser. Photographs of all of her dogs lined the back of the dresser. Several floral prints in wide gilt frames adorned the wall. Stuck inside the edges of the frames were wallet-sized school photos of nieces and nephews. A floral housecoat hung on the back of the bedroom door. A bottle of "Evening in Paris" cologne stood on her nightstand.

AS HER EYESIGHT AND PHYSICAL strength diminished, Mimi's inner core strengthened. On rare days, like today, I greeted her sitting in her recliner with her head bowed and her hands across her eyes. "A bad one, eh?" I asked.

We had no secrets. None since that day Mimi had taught me to crochet. It wasn't the skill that I learned. My scarves and other small, hand-made items were poorly constructed with uneven stitches and often were wider at one end than the other. But my insides became more settled. I learned how to channel the stuff of dread, uneasiness, and foreboding into something productive. I learned I was bigger than my shyness, my awkwardness, my demons. Now, we were more like contemporaries.

"The food here stinks," she frowned.

"I'm picking you up for dinner on Sunday. That's just two days from today." I knew how much my aunts missed home-cooked food, Italian food. The aides were good caregivers, but not Italian cooks.

"Good. That's good. I'll get a decent meal then. Last night it was frozen fish sticks and breaded okra. Can you believe it?" she snorted. "And, not even hot. They should be ashamed! I told the aide she ought to learn how to cook. C-O-O-K." She spelled it slowly, emphatically.

"How about I take you and Elna out for lunch later?"

"Nope. Not up to it." She vented. "And what's with the rest of the family?"

"Didn't Keith, your nephew, call you Sunday?"

"That was days ago. You'd think we had fallen off the edge of the earth."

"We'll call Sunday from my house."

"There's no excuse for this."

"I'm sure you're right." I knew my aunt was lonely and frightened. Fearful because Elna's cancer had spread. I looked at Mimi's hands: "Maybe later you'll want a manicure."

"Where's my Alfred Dunner blouse? The one with the cathedral print with all the bright colors? I can't find it." Her face grew sour.

"I'll look in your closet."

"Not there." She sat forward, leaning on the arms of her chair, "I may be blind, but I know my clothes." Her macular degeneration had left just a pinprick of light in each eye, but she had learned to accommodate her disability. After all, she had learned to live with just one lung, her demons, and a recent hip replacement.

I jumped up, "I'm looking right now."

"Found it!" I returned with the wrinkled blouse in hand. "In the hamper."

"Did you check Pretty Boy's cage for food?"

"Yes, it's fine. Cage is clean, fresh newspaper on the bottom." Since they were no longer able to walk small dogs, their pets had become a succession of lime-green parakeets. The birds were let out of the cage, allowed to fly around the apartment. They took particular delight in perching on the frame of Elna's glasses. "Pretty Boy, Pretty Boy," Mimi whistled and the bird flew to the top of the bookshelf then settled on the back of her chair.

"You look good in red. You ought to wear it more often," Mimi gestured toward my red sweater.

"Thanks."

"So, how are you?"

"Oh, you know. Busy with the house, visiting Dad, keeping up with the boys and then there's the garden."

"You're too young to be alone. For God's sake, get out once in a while." I smiled at her as she patted the armrest for emphasis.

"Oh, I just haven't found anyone I am interested in yet."

"Well, I'm not suggesting you get married. Just dinner, just something easy, simple. *Fun*." Henry had been dead five years. I had not had a date since his death.

"I'll think about it."

"You sit around long enough like me, you'll rust. Get a life!"

It was different than I imagined. It was peaceful, simple, quiet, not the end that Mimi had feared. Mimi was lying in her gray polyester slacks and her good Alfred Dunner, cathedral-print blouse, wearing a pair of black loafers. Her nails were neatly manicured and her hair was combed softly around her face. The aide tipped back her blue recliner. Mimi's eyes were closed and her breathing was very, very shallow.

"She is in a coma. It won't be long now." The aide touched my arm lightly: "But your aunt is strong. You never know." She smiled at me: "That's why I called you right away. I knew you'd want to be here. I'll be in the kitchen if you need me." She disappeared. I looked back to say something but found I had no words. I pulled up a chair to sit as closely as possible to my aunt, remembering her request: "Be here. Promise me. I don't want to die alone."

The year before, Mimi had stayed in her recliner in the living room while Elna was in her bedroom dying and refused to see her sister. Through the whole vigil, she was terrified — not by what happens after death (she was a believer), but because she knew how cruel and unforgiving life in the body was. "I don't want to see her like that. I have my last memory of her. *You go.*"

She had watched so many people she loved suffer: her sister and her father with stomach cancer, Grandma and Maribel living with dementia in nursing homes, her brother Joe, so many friends. Most of her family were dead. She who had been so afraid, so hesitant (who said she never quite understood what life was about), had outlived nearly everyone, exhibiting a grit that people admired. When complimented on her strengths, she just looked back with her half-blind eyes, "What? Me? You're kidding! You have no idea how scared I am of this life."

I leaned forward and whispered in my aunt's ear, "Mimi. Mimi. I'm here. I am here now." Her breath continued to slow.

"I know you can hear me. I won't leave you. I'll stay."

And so I sat with my beloved aunt, hearing only muffled sounds from the kitchen, and an occasional sparrow chirping in the oak tree outside the window. It had come to this, the gift of a peaceful death. The death certificate would read "Old Age" under "cause of death."

A little melody hummed in the space between my ribs. I felt a sort of contentment that Mimi had left her body so easily. Mimi, who could barely walk, had raised her hips to leap over that last hurdle, surmounting the final barrier.

"Everything that slows us down and forces patience,
everything that sets us back into the slow circles of nature,
is a help. Gardening is an instrument of grace."
– May Sarton

When I began this journey, I had no idea that I would make a
complete circle, leaving Sweet Woods Garden and going halfway
around the world to return to my garden. I am walking May
Sarton's "slow circles of nature." I left my garden in early spring
and returned later that year when the day lilies and Oriental pop-
pies produced blooms. At the top of the hill, I could see the poppies
in full bloom, their red-orange petals falling open, revealing ink-
black centers.

I do have a favorite flower. It's the Oriental poppies, but I
have never said so out loud or acknowledged it to the garden. My
attachment to flowers seems silly, fierce, emotional. Yet somehow
I feel that if I acknowledge a favorite, the others in the garden
might become jealous, not bloom, not grow. I know my garden has
that energy. My boys would often look at each other with raised
eyebrows when I returned to the house after working hours in the
garden – dirty, sweaty, happy, "You were gardening all this time,
Mom?" "Oh," I would say, "there were other things to do," and the
boys would give me their "whatever" expressions.

I remember those fierce rivalries between childhood friends. The
terrible combination of three, three friends. Two was perfect bal-
ance, or four (two pairs of two), but three seemed to set up rivalries,
competition in which one girl always felt left out, rejected, less. Not
Enough. The memory of that competition from my childhood nearly
brings tears to my eyes. I close my eyes and feel them smart and my

fists clench with the vivid memory (now nearly fifty-five-years old) that my best friend Penny could possibly have chosen Janet instead of me.

As an adult, I can't play those games. I don't play them. I couldn't bear to be disappointed that way again. My garden is full of a variety of flowers and I tend them all, yet sometimes when I sneak up the hill to take in the beauty of a just-opening poppy, I feel the delphinium and the columbine eye me jealously like that triad of children. Such rivalry in my peaceful garden!

SWEET WOODS GARDEN IS MY COMMITMENT. I am bound to it. It is best that I don't argue with the plants and the place of the graves in my life. Best I pay attention. After all, the five are doing more for me dead than they ever could have alive. What I hadn't understood was that my contract with them was as never ending as my commitment to the garden. When I die, I will join them in this contract. I will do for those I leave behind what the five have done for me.

There is no getting out of this, ever, not in present time, not in the afterlife. I am bound. *Bound by love, by commitment.* Bound to those spirits as easily as I am to the task of staking peonies, securing the tall, heavy blossoms, allowing the flowers to reach maturity before dying back to the ground each year. The early spring peonies' fragrant blooms open by Mother's Day. The heavy flowers require staking. I know I ought to be ruthless, removing the side buds to allow the main flowers to grow larger, but I am greedy for as many flowers as the plants will bear and settle for multiple, smaller blooms. I will stand at my dining room picture window eager for their beauty, their color, and the pleasure they give. I will feel like the small child I had been, peering with my aunts into the gaily decorated Christmas window on Chicago's State Street, watching animated figures ice skate across circles of mirrored glass.

Just as easily and naturally as I had put caps and sweaters on my kids when they were infants, I find myself nurturing my plants. Winter's last heavy coat of frost melts and the first few days of spring bring bold sunshine to the back garden, the hottest spot on the property. There, the Japanese peonies will poke bright red buds of hope through winter's decay.

The former owner of the house (a tree person) had planted the flowers in the wrong place and the wrong soil. Shade and clay. I moved them, digging up the enormous clumps of roots carefully, prayerfully, splitting the roots and setting them three feet apart in larger holes, gently covering their bare roots with manure and compost. The following spring I watched breathlessly as red buds surfaced in proper sunlight, growing back from the root into bushy green plants sending out profuse bloom. The show, unfolding from the window, in mountain sunlight so bright that it warms my hands just as my aunts' hands warmed mine as we gazed at the magic of Marshall Field's Christmas windows.

In mid-May, I would bring in my first buckets of pink and white blooms, some of them six inches across, petals soft as feathers. Just two flowers filled my huge Japanese ceramic bowl, lingering there for several days grateful to be released from the soft stems that bent with the weight of the flowers pulling the plant nearly to the ground.

I had often visited my Grandmother Belle, my mother's mother, in early spring as a child. Grandma Belle was a tidy housekeeper, yet she delighted in bringing her massive peonies into the parlor, setting those pink and white flowers in pitchers on the round, pie-crust-edged, mahogany table. It was the only time she did not fret about ants in the house. The scent of the flowers perfumed her parlor. Whenever I have pitchers of the blooms in my own home, I think how her past flowers into my present.

I had looked forward to this trip all summer, my return to China, a country that fits my skills and my nature like a good marriage. I had been invited to work at the same hospital where John had been a patient, pulling out old skills from earlier years as a medical social worker. This time, I would be working in a hospital where no kin of mine were in pain. None of my relatives is dying or needing to live with me for rehabilitation or needing me to find housing for them in an assisted living center. That was all behind me.

The next fourteen hours on a jumbo jet would be my mini-vacation, my respite, before ten-hour work days began. I had gathered this gift of idle time with no tasks, no chores, and no obligations. It was my party and I intended to begin celebrating as soon as I boarded. *The next fourteen hours are gifts. I will spread this time like presents on my lap, open each package slowly, let the pleasure of this time wash over me like a balm, enjoy the minutes of each hour, and remain anonymous to fellow passengers. I will open the bag of comfort items placed on my seat, 7F, remove my shoes, pull out the travel socks and drape the blue lap blanket over my legs. I will recline my seat, slide the window shades down, close my eyes and fade into a hazy place where dreams surface.*

On my way to board I passed a girl in a wheelchair near the gate. I tried to avert my eyes. But it was too late. I saw her and her image stuck in my mind. A small, gray cloud floated across my sunny day. I tried to blink away the sight of a young Chinese girl confined to a wheelchair. *Not your job. Not going there.*

A man and woman circled this Chinese girl dressed in jeans, a tee and sneakers. These adults hovered over her chair, their bodies taut, brittle, as if their limbs had been stretched too far and they were veering off a precipice. Their faces were drawn and their skin raw, chaffed by the girl's wounds. *That was me last year. That was me, with the wild, panicked look I see today in the woman's eyes.*

The girl had slipped down in the chair. Her pushed-up pant leg exposed the tube strapped to it, filled with urine. A newsboy cap was skewed on her head at an angle, quite possibly to hide her face from stares and public humiliation. From what I knew of Chinese culture, the people with her were family members, probably her parents.

I blinked again. *Not your job.* I saw other passengers avert their eyes as they walked past her wheelchair. I could hear my mother's voice cautioning me when, as an eight-year-old child, my tiny buds of compassion were flowering: "Don't stare. You'll make them feel uncomfortable." I tried not to gape or gawk, but I could not deny my own wounds. I was stuck with my ache as I walked forward in line to board. I continued to move forward, but my feet sank into the tightly packed clay of despair just below the surface of my past.

I blinked and saw my oldest son, just one year ago, in a wheelchair at this same gate. I could see his nightmare and mine – no recovery, no progress, no change. It was dead calm inside this memory and I couldn't look at the lovely, broken Chinese girl who was just my son's age without sinking further.

My mouth was dry, a kind of dread-dry that no water can quench. My tongue thickened as years of my son's pain worked their way up from my gut. I was walking into my son's life, or what was left of it, after the seizure that caused the fall that broke his foot and led to complications that had left the rest of his life shattered, and mine, too. He had left his job, his apartment and school at twenty-five to become his mother's child again. Then after years of failed treatments for pain, he had made his desperate trip to China.

The line crept forward. I stepped inside the plane and smelled the stale air of my son's closed bedroom, his closed life. I reached my designated seat, turned on the air vent above me and sucked in cool air.

The Chinese family boarded accompanied by a stewardess who spoke Chinese. They should have boarded first, so I saw that this process of flying on an American airline was new to them. They seemed overwhelmed as they looked up and down rows trying to find seat numbers, lost in a maze of American engineering. I wondered if the girl's illness was also new to them. They didn't have that resigned look yet. I watched the mother and saw the girl's face as the cap came off and noticed how alike they looked. The relationship was clear. *She was a looker, a charmer, a dazzler, a knockout. Now she's just a throwaway, damaged goods.* I blinked and saw all the failed drugs and treatments in my own son's life.

Wouldn't you just know it? This aircraft seats four hundred passengers and this family is seated in my row. I felt a sly smile form on the surface of guilt that floated across my consciousness and I heard a small voice say: *Talk with them. Tell them.* But another voice did not want to let them know I was a medical social worker going to China, did not want to tell them that I am the mother of a disabled child. I wanted my time – *my version* of this trip, *not this.*

I closed my eyes and pretended disinterest. I heard the words "*nuér*," Chinese for "daughter," uttered between the man and woman as they busied themselves covering her up to her neck with blankets. I could hear the doctors at the hospital cautioning my son when he wanted to crank air conditioning way up in the summer, "Don't chill your qi." The parents reached above the girl's head and turned off the cold air jets. I reached up and turned mine down.

The mother replaced the cap on her daughter's head, pulling it low over her eyes, and whispered something I could not hear into her daughter's ear. The father stood in the aisle beside the girl's seat, his face a mask, save his eyes that were two black holes of grief. The mother spoke softly to her daughter, cradled one of her listless hands between both of hers, and rocked back and forth. She blotted her daughter's face with wet cloths and offered her orange juice from a cup, holding the straw in her mouth so she could suck. The father looked warily up and down the aisle, saw that the aisle was clear, reached below his daughter's pant leg and drained the urine from the tube into the empty water bottle in his hands, his face as sour as the task. I tried to look away as he slipped into the bathroom to empty it.

I settled into my seat, reached for the novel I had wanted to read all summer. I opened it and the words floated off the page because I was not reading it. I was hiding. I placed the novel in my seat pocket. I burrowed in my blanket and pretended that this tiny lap blanket was doing its job and would comfort me. Yet the pain this family was feeling had been dangled before my consciousness. I remember wanting something to get me through when my son was flying halfway around the world for treatment.

I slid further down in the blanket and turned on my side, attempting to face away from what was next to me. I wanted to slide away, sleep. *They don't want to speak with me, a stranger, an American. Chinese are private, especially about family. They aren't like Americans who splatter their personal lives across channels of reality television, eager to confess their faults as if public confession is some contemporary form of prayer.* I shifted in my seat unable to find a comfortable position.

What are you afraid to lose by speaking with them? If I asked for my seat to be relocated I would violate something sacred within me. I thought about my son, who was better since he went to China for healing. This year, for the first time in his adult life, neither of us was bound by his pain.

"I'm going to need a translator," I heard myself saying in a voice I barely recognized to the stewardess as she passed.

As soon as the stewardess explained that I was a medical person on my way to a major teaching hospital in China, the woman became undone. She reached across the armrest between us, hugged me to her. Her mask of control crumbled and she wept and chattered rapidly in Chinese. The stewardess told me that her daughter had been a graduate student at an American university, a scholar, a straight A student, until she developed a mysterious fever following an infection, and then paralysis. But the reason really didn't matter. The woman continued to cry and hug me. Our faces were pressed cheek to cheek, her tears spilling onto my neck and down my arms. My own eyes filled. I felt her body shudder with grief.

I held her for nearly an hour as the pain she must have held back during all of her trip to America flowed like an untapped source of fresh spring water, baptizing us both. I peered over to her husband and saw the edges of his mouth curl into the smallest of smiles. He nodded. I nodded in return. I stilled my body. I was this woman's solace, holding her, not daring to move, barely daring to breathe. I wanted to absorb this elegant gift, this moment of grace I did not deserve. *She is me. I am her. We are each other. She is my mirror.*

The stewardess faded away. We no longer needed words. We were just two mothers unbound, loosening ourselves. We were simply two moms, comrades, friends.

I WAS SIXTY-FIVE-YEARS OLD, stiff, sore, and working full time as a social worker for the first time in twenty-eight years. I was putting in a sixty-hour work week at the First Teaching Hospital of Tianjin and it was taking its toll. Yet I was eager for the challenge, and my gratitude for the invitation to this country was as bright as the red quilt I threw off my legs. I ought to have been dressing, but first I wandered to the window, cranked it open and looked down from the tenth floor of the apartment that would be home for the next six weeks.

I looked out on a city of eleven million people. Across from me a Chinese woman was watering her garden on the eighth floor rooftop, a green patch against a gray, smoggy sky, above seven lanes of noisy traffic. She bent over, tending each potted plant individually and as if they were children, pressing her finger tenderly into the soil, testing, checking. She hovered over several larger pots. *Is her garden like mine?*

She had filled precious space with *plants* when it could have been *living* space. She had made this conscious choice. She was tending a gourd with spreading tendrils, a symbol of fertility. *Her garden. My garden.* I smiled at her and wished she would look up so I could wave. She didn't see me. I waved anyway.

On the sidewalk below, the local barber was setting up his simple shop – a straight-backed wooden chair at the edge of the curb. He sat on the chair, patted his pocket, pulled out a black comb and scissors, stood, placed them on the chair, and picked up a broom and sheet. He swept the area around the chair, making it tidy for his first customer whose hair would litter the sidewalk. As he shook out the white sheet he used for a drape, I could almost hear it snap like my mother's sheets after she pulled them off the line in the backyard.

Am I really on the other side of the world? This transition from my home in the United States is so familiar, so easy. It feels like a second home, this place that engages me so.

Further down the street, a small group of adults were gently doing Tai Chi exercises, their slow, graceful movements such a contrast to the traffic whizzing by. The bicycle repairman would soon unlock his tiny hut on the corner. These huts appeared throughout the city where repairmen serviced the thousands of bicycles in transit. Bicyclists could get tires patched or a broken chain replaced on their way to work. Inside the hut the repairman had a variety of bicycle maintenance supplies and the skills to do nearly any job in minutes.

I dressed quickly and scolded myself for lingering at the window, staring as if I was a six-year-old at the circus for the first time. When the invitation came to live and work in the third largest city in China, I said, "Of course." I didn't pause.

"When do you need me?" When in my life had I ever left my home for six weeks? I had property to care for, kids, family, stuff. But it just felt right. I needed this trip. I needed it to gather myself, lay the foundation for those things necessary to sow a new life. That's how I described it to my family. That's all I knew. The trip to China would confirm all I believed about Sweet Woods Garden.

I especially remember the last day of my ten-day visit two years earlier when John was a patient in this same city. I stood at an open casement window similar to the one I had just opened. That window was just beyond John's room, at the end of the hallway on the hospital's twelfth floor. I tried to hold back tears of what felt like a terrible separation from this city I had come to feel was my second home. I wanted to overload my senses with it all – the noise from the lanes of traffic below me, the sight of construction cranes everywhere and buildings springing up overnight in this metropolis, the smell of smog that lingered until late morning. I had said that I hated big cities, never wanted to live in one again once I left Chicago after fifty years of winters, traffic, and taxes. Yet there I stood.

I spoke little Chinese. I learned a word a day from my driver on the short ride to work. Angela and Samanda, young Chinese bilingual staff members at the office across from the hospital, taught me a few basic words. They had prepared an index card for me to carry in my backpack when I traveled alone. The card had my apartment address on one side and the address of the hospital on the other. With this system, I traveled seamlessly, silently, through the city not needing to speak much. It almost felt as if less was expected of me because I was not fluent. I allowed myself this luxury and became a passive observer in my own life. Outside my work with Americans and international English-speaking patients, my limited Chinese allowed me this gift of silence. I absorbed everything around me like a sponge.

The rhythm of this place carried me where I needed to be. I walked the neighborhood near my apartment building at night without fear, jumped into tiny Chinese cabs and crossed the city unafraid. Conversation consisted of hand gestures, smiles, and liberal use of my index card, so unlike my noisy life in the United States. I floated around, effervescent, radiating a peacefulness I had not known, feeling a sort of *déja vu*.

At the entrance to First Teaching Hospital, rows and rows of bicycles were tightly lined up along the curb. Each day that I went to work, I saw the same old woman collect a handful of coins, her payment, from bicyclists who parked there. This woman, in a traditional gray, Mao jacket and dusty, faded black pants, had a lucrative business. Her lined brown face revealed that she worked outside all year long. Samanda and Angela called it "farmer's skin," undesirable in this country. "Farmer's skin" means "peasant." White skin means "affluent city dweller." The girls spent many Yuan from their salaries on whitening creams and wore hats and gloves to cover their arms and heads when they were outdoors and exposed to sunlight.

The bicycle lady had a second business. She kept a fire going in a fifty-gallon drum, its embers hot enough to roast sweet potatoes. People bought their breakfast from her and walked toward the hospital eating steaming sweet potatoes wrapped in brown paper. Each day, I saw her standing next to the fifty-gallon drum, one hand held out to collect coins for the bicycles, the other reaching into the drum with a heavy cotton glove to pull out a hot potato.

Ever mindful, this street woman didn't miss a thing. I felt her eyes swoop past me. One day we eyed each other. I nodded. The next day I eyed her again, bowed slightly. She grinned, giggled, and gave me a toothless smile. The following day I pulled my camera from my backpack. She shook her head vigorously, "*Bu! Bu!*" No! I lowered the camera. She might have believed that taking her picture would steal her soul. I gave her this. After all, she had given me her smile and so I settled for a small room in my mind's eye where I stored this memory.

On my day off, I walked the side streets, awash with smaller, different rhythms, no longer the big, bustling, noisy city, but smaller neighborhoods tucked into the whole. I wandered through narrow streets, tossing down big gulps of China. Handmade wooden carts of all sizes and shapes were parked on the street, packed to the top with fresh peaches, watermelon, and eggplant picked before dawn. A woman selling peaches piled her wagon into a pyramid. I watched her polish each with a small, square cloth. A symbol of long life and good health, a peach tree in the garden means dreams come true. I bought three from her and she handed me the fruit like a gift, bowing slightly, as she looked into my eyes. We spoke without saying a word. I resolved to plant a peach tree in my back yard when I returned to North Carolina.

The tiny noodle shop had only six tables and they took all the space inside the shop. The kitchen was outside on the sidewalk. With a pair of giant chopsticks, the cook dropped noodles he had made from freshly kneaded dough into steaming water. The water was heated in a huge aluminum bowl over a small fire. I pulled out my camera and took his photo. He smiled proudly, and then struck an outlandish pose for a second. He bowed low and grinned. He was younger than the bicycle woman and seemed to have no fear for his soul so I snapped away.

It was mid-summer and the temperature got hot early in the day and didn't cool until after dark, so the shopkeepers left the doors of their narrow shops open. The local flower shop had spilled arrangements onto the sidewalk. Buckets of bird of paradise, stargazer lilies, day lilies, roses in yellow, pink, and orange, and varieties of flowers I had never seen before perfumed the air. I was lightheaded from the intoxicating fragrance and this connection to Sweet Woods Garden. Dragonflies flitted around my head at the shop door. "*Ninhâo,*" I said. "Hello." The shopkeeper peeked her head out the doorway. My tiny attempt at the language was rewarded with her returning "*Ninhâo.*" After speaking that single word I realized that my throat was dry. These were the first words I had spoken in hours. What a pleasure to keep my voice still and communicate only with my eyes, nose, and ears.

Each day before I left the hospital I gazed out of the twelfth-floor windows at the end of the hallway before pressing the elevator button. Today I stood at the windows remembering how I tried to take all of it in on that first visit, fearful I would not return. At that time, I had wished, for the first time in my life, that I was a bigger person physically so I could somehow absorb, suck up more China. More! I wanted bigger eyes, bigger lungs, and a bigger heart to contain the experience. I wanted to super-size myself, although even that would never satisfy me. *So American.*

Behind me, down the long hallway of this international floor just past my son's old room, nurses in their crisp white uniforms were scurrying back and forth. These young women had laid hands on my son again and again during his four-month hospitalization, mothering him when I could not. Dr. Lo, his primary doctor, appeared in the hallway, called to a nurse and they spoke with their heads bowed. This slim, busy doctor had taken time to teach my son Chinese jokes and learn how to laugh again.

Two heads peeked from the housekeeping closet, nodded to me and smiled. Each day, the housekeeping staff cleaned each patient's room, washing the floor by hand. Marshaled in by nurses afterward, four of them deftly pulled the sheets off the bed and snapped the clean ones on tight, each holding a corner. In minutes, the bed was clean and fresh. *Just like Mom.*

It seemed there were hands everywhere. Hands for administering acupuncture twice daily, hands for massage, and hands of the kitchen staff artfully arranging even the simplest vegetable dishes on a tray. *Hands to heal.* And a place to heal and to be touched, just like Sweet Woods Garden, where I feel the soft, silky petals of flowers growing there. It is the same. *Wo dong. I understand. I understand.*

Packed away in my memory is the quote: "Loneliness is the poverty of self, solitude the riches of self." May Sarton, of course. And that feels just right to me. I cannot bear the world constantly pressing against me, taking little chunks of me. I think about the Thanksgiving turkey that sits on my kitchen counter each holiday and how the family picks over it two hours after dinner, always going for the meat closest to the bone, the sweet spot, the most succulent part. I don't mind sharing the juiciest parts of myself, but I also need time to savor my own riches in a quiet space.

It means getting up before my lab awakes, sitting with pen and journal. It means writing down my dreams as soon as I awaken, capturing that marvelous, open space between awake and asleep.

*It means sitting on a cold stone bench in the cemetery in the dark.
It means not blinking when the invitation comes, not arguing
the time, not considering the inconvenience in exchange for the
riches solitude brings.*

*It also means being conscious enough, empty-headed enough,
when the space is offered, to turn my gaze ever so slightly to that
tiny park carved out with four benches sitting just feet away
from a busy Chinese street, a small green space with a few flowers
blooming and the buzz of a dragonfly flitting past. Nothing
vanishes. Nothing.*

IT HAS RAINED, HARD. I walk to the cemetery. Grass brushes
against my garden clogs leaving my feet cold and wet. I make
my way in the dark, flashlight in hand, at three o'clock in the
morning, to Sweet Woods Garden. New spring grass is glow-
ing bright green, nearly neon, against more mature, dark green
blades. A few brown leaves, stragglers from last fall, crunch beneath my feet. I have had a restless night since the telephone
conversation with my oldest son, John. His voice was full of
sorrow, frustration, living on his own in Boston.

Sometimes I am not sure I am enough for this task of . . .
what? Motherhood, for one. I don't have *Enough*. Sometimes
my just being there for my boys and all my careful listening
doesn't seem like *Enough*. I think I have to have all the answers,
forgetting that I have reared competent adults who are capable
of making sound judgments. I lose sight, in my finicky dotage,
of the delight they offer giving back pleasure, living lives I admire and with audacity, courage, and grit. I forget how difficult
it might be for them to be my children. *Get a grip!*

I CLIMBED DOWN THE BASEMENT STEPS in our Chicago home to check on Jason, age four, and his best friend Charlie, a bit nervous since they had been quiet so long. There on the basement floor was a towering castle they had created from their boundless imaginations, a fortress of wooden blocks, a one-time building, a unique piece of architecture. The boys didn't even bother to look my way. They were too lost in their childhood, too engrossed with their castle and their quest, each holding a favorite "Master of the Universe" figure. Jason was holding He-Man, his favorite, the most powerful man in the universe, equipped with his power harness and The Sword of Power. Charlie clutched Man-At-Arms in his fist, his fingers encircling a tiny club in the action figure's hand. Their heroes scaled the wall of the castle and defended the forces of good against evil. The look on their faces told me they were in the midst of the fray. I was just an observer.

They are saving the planet, battling for justice. This is the groundwork for the steadfast friends Jason will keep, the tight friendships he will hold onto through thick and thin. This is fodder for the movie scripts Jason will write as an adult, for his strong sense of ethics as an adult, and for his choice of the spunky woman he will meet.

And John, my "Christmas Kid," who insisted on buying his own sets of Christmas lights with his allowance to string in his bedroom. Although the house was filled with the aroma of the turkey carcass simmering in the kitchen for turkey soup and it was still only Thanksgiving *day*, there was John pushing joy. There was John full of the Christmas spirit, stringing a tangle of lights to remind me to stop, pause, and thank God for the gift of him. As an adult, his compassion for others has been abundant, evident in his loyal friendships and his volunteer work with people with mental illness.

Above me a half-moon rides the star-studded night sky. The wind is gentle but the warm spring weather has turned cold and wintry following a storm. As I enter the garden with its gate blown open, a gust of wind picks up, whips the cuffs of my slacks, and slips beneath the tail of my rain jacket, sending Jack Frost running up my spine.

I walk to the graves and see a depression in the gravel between my parents' markers. "Okay, good," I say, nodding to both of them, checking in. "He'll need that." The indentation is larger than last time. They are opening themselves again to receive John's pain.

I stop at Henry's grave and shine the flashlight toward my feet, running the beam across the name on his marker, *Henry William Gunther Lauritzen*. "He needs you now," is all I can think to say (as if I need to tell him what he already knows). I step back and turn off the light: "I know you're doing your job. I just don't know sometimes how to do *mine*."

I turn from the five graves and walk to the crape myrtle tree, symbol of love and immortality, the tree where the raccoon died as a sacrifice to the garden, where I reconnect to myself, to the strength of others. I didn't know its meaning when I planted this tree, what it symbolized, or did I, somewhere inside myself? After all I have experienced, I am no longer a believer in random events.

The wind gains strength as I approach the tree. I put my flashlight down on the stone bench to my left, step next to the tree, grasp the lower branches, place my forehead on a third limb to get as much of my body as possible in contact with the tree. Tears spill onto the limb, the intensity of my need surprising me.

"Let John know he is strong and can rise above this." My hands tighten around the limbs.

I feel the vibration from within the living, breathing energy of this tree. The wind howls around me. I feel the tree sway and I bend with the rhythm of it. Earth energy pulses through my clogs, travels through my body, then flows back into the tree. I am looping over and over and swaying, almost dancing, in this cycle of energy. I look up into the branches of the crape myrtle that stretch into the night sky. I gaze at the moon and stars and white puffs of clouds illuminated by moonlight shining down on me. I stare at my hands. They are holding the limbs of the branches of the tree in a V. Of course! The V of the tree has become the fork of my dowsing rod. I am divining my life, understanding my stories, divining myself, touching the sacred. I empty out all of my inadequacies, my *Not Enoughs*, with the whoosh of a deep sigh. I am dousing the fire of my *Not Enoughs* with an exhalation of my breath.

This place! This place centers me, brings me back to who I am. The five keep me honest, keep me true.

I see myself as a young girl, maybe nine years old, delighting in the joy of a surprise birthday gift from my father. Dad was forty-five. His hair slicked back, smelling of Vitalis, glistened blue-black in the August sunlight. We were sitting in the grass in the front yard admiring a dollhouse that he had built in his basement workshop for my birthday. We peered into the tiny windows of the dollhouse. It was a replica of our two-story home. I turned the tiny, wooden end tables over in my hands and noted how alike they were to those in our living room, the ones that, until now, I had thought dull and uninteresting. Now that they were in my house and they were *my* furniture, they didn't look half bad.

"Where do you think this should go?" Dad handed me a carved, ivory-colored sofa. I took the tiny piece of furniture from his hands, shifted the end tables and arranged my living room to suit my taste. "How about this?" Dad handed me a bed and a tiny, white bedside table. I placed it on the second floor of the house replicating my bedroom.

I realize now that my parents had worked as partners on this birthday project. Mom had let my friends' mothers know to buy the dollhouse furniture as gifts and Dad had created my own little home. The best of them was right there, right then. My parents had put all the goodness of their relationship into that doll house. All that had worked in their marriage they handed me that day.

And this moment here in Sweet Woods Garden. It is almost as if this memory whispers *Enough.* They had given me *Enough* to nurture my own beginning buds of motherhood. I am *Enough.*

My fingers relax and my body turns on its axis, centered, whole, strong.

I return to the garden.

To Sweet Woods Garden.

Always the garden.

Nothing vanishes.
Nothing.

About the Author

Before becoming an author Karen Lauritzen worked as a medical social worker in many agencies or organizations, including an in-home health care team caring for the elderly, dying and disabled, a dialysis center, a day center with schizophrenic patients, settlement houses and agencies aiding the Jewish community. In  her sixties she returned to work in Tianjin, China at the invitation of the hospital where her oldest son had been a patient.

She writes short stories, poetry and essays. Her work has been published in *The Chrysalis Reader*, *WNC-Woman Magazine*, *Kaleidoscope Magazine: Exploring the Experience of Disability through the Fine Arts* and *Women's Spaces, Women's Places*, an anthology of women writers. One of the stories from *Nothing Vanishes: Memoir of a Life Transformed*, "Seat 7F," won an honorary mention in the 2010 *Carpe Articulum* Literary Awards.

She lives in Brevard, North Carolina. This is her first book.

Acknowledgments

Many people, far more than I mention here, helped make this book. Those listed here are but a few:

Peggy Tabor Millin, master teacher, helped me find my voice.

Kevin "Mc" McIlvoy, took me to the abyss and helped me find my vision.

Editor Karen Schaffer and photographer Pamela Blevins spent countless hours searching for right words and pictures.

Book and cover designer Ginger Graziano described herself as a "visual spokesperson" for her clients. She's more than that. She's an alchemist.

Videographers Accem Scott and Tracey Schmidt made a book trailer that truly reflects Sweet Woods Garden and its sense of place in my life.

To Marne and Dennis Sutton for their generous support, kind words and enthusiasm for my work.

CPSIA information can be obtained
at www.ICGtesting.com
Printed in the USA
FFOW01n1647140515
13368FF

9 780985 859503